CONTENTS

DEDICATION

This book is dedicated to the P-N's.
For having faith in me to go out and make stuff happen.
Love you.

INTRODUCTION

Anna Parker-Naples is on a mission to help purpose-led, ambitious entrepreneurs, experts, creatives & coaches amplify their message, to be seen and heard by the people who need their help.

As the author of international bestseller *Get Visible* & now *Podcast with Impact* she is doing exactly that.

Anna is driven to help emerging, aspiring and established leaders to tap into their unlimited potential and be exceptional at what they do.

This is the ripple effect that can change the world.

One podcast listener at a time.

PODCASTING IS POWERFUL

Podcasting *is* powerful

It offers huge opportunities to experts, authors, coaches, speakers and entrepreneurs to increase impact, influence and income for their brand. It is a medium that is growing at an unprecedented level with audience figures that were anticipated to double in size over an 18 month period. This was accelerated by the recent pandemic.

Done effectively, podcasts can build email lists, audience followings and create strong communities. A podcast can be a real asset in your efforts to bring in loyal clients and elevate your status within your industry.

Done ineffectively, and without crucial knowledge,

it can become a headache and something you wonder why you started. I don't want that for you.

Anyone who is anyone in the online business space right now is moving towards launching a podcast. It is fast becoming the best way to educate, inspire and connect with potential and current clients as listeners go about their daily lives. A podcast takes effort and I want to help you ensure that your show works well for you right from the word go. I want to empower you to create a show that doesn't get lost in the noisy online space. Get the planning right, and your podcast will be an invaluable tool for driving sales and adding additional income streams to your business.

Knowledge is key in launching a successful, profitable podcast and in this book I will take you from aspiring podcaster to informed, confident podcast host. I will give you the best chance of launching a podcast that works for you and your business. With solid foundations, your podcast can grow to heady heights, taking you and your personal brand quickly in the direction of leadership in your chosen area of expertise or passion.

Chapters include detailed advice on how to plan, prepare, record, edit and launch your podcast. I'll be drawing on my experience of hosting two podcasts - one released quietly under the radar without a clue about how to launch or leverage a podcast for my business ... the other with insider knowledge, experience and a commitment to making the show as well-received and popular as possible. I'll bring to the table a wealth of audio experience as a multi-award-winning audio producer and voice actor, together with entrepreneurial knowledge from running a highly profitable online business. The aim is for you to be confident, in control and informed about the recording and editing process.

Podcasting isn't just plugging in a microphone and putting out any old voice recording. Rather, it is an important mechanism for leaders - aspiring, emerging and established - to get their message heard by the right ears. This is how we can reach people who need us to lift, inspire, motivate, transform, entertain and educate them. This is how we create our ripple effect.

Right now, hosting a podcast is the best way to make a solid impact as a key figure within your industry. Podcasting allows you to put your stamp all over your niche, to be known for what you do, to get your business out there visibly and position you as a credible expert in your field of influence. It has the potential to open doors in a way no other platform can.

Since I've been podcasting I have been asked to appear on countless podcasts as a guest. I've reached audiences of millions and been invited to speak at high-profile events I couldn't have accessed in any other way. I've built relationships by making deep, lasting connections and collaborations with people that I've invited on to my own podcast. You'll find out for yourself that having guests on your show will open up your own networks to influential people in a way no other medium can.

Statistics

You may think statistics are dry but these will be a wake-up call as to why you need to make podcasting work for you.

First – who is listening to podcasts? Who tunes in whilst doing chores at home? Exercising? Driving? According to Ofcom at the end of 2019, 7.1 million people in the UK listen to podcasts each week. If we look across the world, South Korea has the highest listenership at 54%. Here in the UK approximately 18% of the population listens regularly. In the US, it's 34%. When you consider that one in eight people here in the UK are listening to podcasts, and over a third in the US, it is clear that this is a popular and thriving field you should not neglect. The podcast industry is growing year on year and is predicted to double in listenership between 2020 and 2022. In most countries that will mean over half the population will be tuning in to the content they love.

And podcasting isn't quite the newfangled platform

you might think it is. It has actually been around for 15 years, although in its current form, where we can find it easily on our mobile phones, it's about six years old. According to leaders from *Google* and *Spotify* speaking at a recent podcast event expectations are that the industry will continue to accelerate for the foreseeable future. Big corporations are ploughing investment into the industry and technology to ensure they don't miss out on this valuable market.

Many small business owners I speak with fear that the podcast market is becoming flooded, so I find these predictions exciting. Giants like *Spotify*, *Google* and *Apple* consider podcasting to be in its infancy, comparable in many ways to the early years in television, and creators are experimenting with form and ways to create. We know that podcasting has already grown as a powerful influencing platform. Think about most of the social influencers or business leaders you follow online. Most will have their own podcast, or if not yet, utilize podcast guesting to expand their influence. By starting your own show now you'll be a relatively early adopter, better able to position yourself as a market leader and trailblazer than those who never get started or wait several years to enter the podcast space.

Half of all listeners have begun listening within the last two years. New listeners are coming on to the platforms in droves looking for quality content and actively searching for great material on a worldwide scale. It's astonishing to be able to track the popularity of your podcast episodes in far flung corners of the world, places you've never dreamed of visiting, with fans consuming content on a regular basis. That's the beauty of audio content - it reaches places you and your business ordinarily can't.

In April 2020 the podcasting world hit the milestone of one million live podcasts globally. Not all of those podcasters are creating content on a regular, weekly basis. Some shows might still be hosted and available to listen to, but their creators are not producing and releasing new episodes. When you think of *YouTube* and its 31+ million channels, this is a tiny number. Podcasts are just getting started. And when you break down shows into countries, regions, topics, languages, categories and niches it transpires that you don't have as much competition as you may have at first assumed. Additionally, many of the shows already out there don't have as good quality audio content as you're going to learn how to create through this book. When you do your research into competitor shows later on, you'll be astounded at how poor some of them are. Not yours, though. At least not on my watch.

Listener Behaviour

Listeners tend to be loyal to the shows they love. They return again and again to the podcasts that inspire, educate and entertain them most. Right now people are listening on average to six shows they have subscribed to and opted in to have that show's new episodes displayed in their podcast feed automatically, ready to be downloaded in their podcast app of preference.

Including those six shows they're listening to approximately seven episodes per week, so it can be assumed that they're consuming as much material as they can of that particular show. This also indicates that there is room for something new in their line-up and people are actively looking for new shows to listen to. This is where you come in. If people are looking for a new show, they won't find you and your expertise if you aren't there will they? Instead, they'll turn to your competition.

Content consumption

In a recent study by *Edison Research* on *The Podcast Consumer 2019*, it was found that 80% of listeners play through all or most of an episode. They are engaged. This is unlike video content where the majority of viewers drop off before reaching the 10-25% mark. Consumer knowledge like this is important if you are thinking of monetizing your podcast through sponsorship or affiliations, or through promoting your own work, services, events or products. Listeners generally trust the podcast host and feel connected to the show. We can assume that people drop off towards the latter part of the episode because whatever they are doing whilst listening - the commute, exercise session, housework - is complete, rather than lack of interest in the topic.

Worldwide, the majority of podcast listeners come from incomes of over $60,000 USD per household and tend to be educated beyond standard school leaver age. Whilst this will shift as funding is made available to support and reach those audiences currently underserved and under-represented, the majority of current podcast listeners are affluent and educated, with money to invest in luxuries and learning. For your business, this is important.

How listeners are tuning in will be imperative to understand when we look later at how you will create your show. Understanding people's time slots and activities will inform the content you create. 49% of people listen at home – perhaps in the shower, whilst cooking dinner or getting dressed in the morning. People are listening not just with earbuds whilst doing household activities but are increasingly connected to their smart speakers - also seeing massive growth. Podcast listening is taking place in the background. As we do things that aren't terribly interesting we're educating and entertaining ourselves.

It's important to note that 22% of people listen in the car or whilst commuting by train or bus. Knowing this informs the length of the show you will create. Think about when people have an opportunity to listen. In the podcast that I'm currently hosting, *Entrepreneurs Get Visible*, most episodes are short and snappy because my listener tends to tune in during that 10-15 minute slot where they have short bursts of time. Perhaps they're taking the children to school, have a limited commute or a window of opportunity before their next client meeting. My content is designed to fit these small pockets of time. Whatever you create must have your ideal listener in mind.

Visibility and Association

A successful podcast launch can lead to greater collaboration within your business area and increased popularity for your show. In the few years I've been podcasting I have had incredible guests on my shows. I have forged collaborations where we've gone on to partner in some way or be affiliates for each other's programs. Better than that, I have elevated my own status within my industry, raised my own game – all as a result of networking and having deep, connected conversations with more established peers and leaders than I would ordinarily be able to access. The reason? Experts, leaders, authors and successful entrepreneurs want to come on my show because they want to get in front of my audience. Both before and after the official interview slot, we have the opportunity to chat and build rapport and foundations for a solid connection so valuable for business. Not to mention the friendships that have blossomed, a wonderful by-product of having in-depth one-on-one conversations. Podcast hosting enables you to grow your business - not just in terms of awareness of what you do and who you are as a key person of influence. If done well it can make a difference in the quality and quantity of potential clients who join your mailing list, your community ... who want to work with you, become your clients, buy your services, buy your products. The all-important *know like and trust* factor is crucial to effective marketing. That holy grail is much more achievable when you deliver good quality podcast content on a regular, consistent basis. I've said it before and no doubt I'll say it again in this book: *podcasting is powerful.*

Podcasting increases your business visibility. In my book *Get Visible: How to have more Impact, Influence and*

Income I focus on the importance of *visibility* ... on people knowing who you are and what you're all about. Many of us have businesses, missions, purposes and a sense of calling. We have the ability to transform lives - inspire, educate, lift and motivate. Visibility matters because it is key to increasing your impact, influence and income. Your own show gives you the commitment to be consistent with your message and your marketing simply by having pertinent conversations.

Podcasting allows for increased search-ability. Podcast directories such as *Spotify* and *iTunes* are akin to powerful search engines. For every single guest that appears on your show, your name and the shows that you have been connected with as a guest, and the shows that your guests have been connected with, are then linked. Choose your guests strategically and you and your brand will be positioned alongside them. Be intentional about who you invite on as a guest and enjoy an increased organic audience as a result, especially when your show is promoted within *iTunes*, *Spotify* and *Google* as a recommendation for listeners.

A podcast also allows you to create ample social media content opportunities to alleviate the concern of 'What the hell should I write?!" that so often accompanies the demands of posting on social media for brand awareness. It positions you as someone with expertise and enables you to email your list with relevant, useful information that answers their biggest problems. Hosting a podcast makes connecting with your audience easier and more purposeful.

Common Objections to Podcasting

I hear some common objections from people considering starting a podcast. Let's address those excuses now. In doing so, I hope that when you encounter overwhelm around creating your show you will push on through and get your show launched rather than allow it to be another idea that didn't quite happen. Someone needs to hear your message. MANY people need to hear your message!

'I'm too busy.'

A lot of potential podcasters tell me they're too busy for a podcast. They believe the myth that running a show would be time-consuming. In truth, a podcast is a way to make *best* use of your time. Consider this, for example: by creating a *Facebook Live* video with high quality audio for your community, you have something you can turn into a podcast episode. You can use a transcription service to create show notes that could be revised into a separate blogpost. From there, you could upload the content into a *YouTube* video and post the video on *LinkedIn, Instagram* or *IGTV*. Suddenly, one piece of content has the potential to reach tens of thousands and all you've done is flicked on that microphone and recorded yourself speaking. And you can make sure your podcast works for *you* ... I make mine fit into other commitments. I have created material whilst out walking my dog in the quiet fields nearby. I tell the listeners: 'This is what I'm doing today. This is where I am.' Content is integrated into my everyday life. I've recorded episodes whilst on stage giving a talk and have repurposed that speech into my podcast. In many ways, podcasting is about creating *more* time for yourself. If you want to be seen as an expert in your field, you'll be creating content anyway, such as videos, blogposts and articles. Podcasting speeds up and intensifies the whole process.

'I'm a technophobe.'

Some people tell me they're worried that podcasts are too technical and they have no interest in that. As you'll find out later I have vast audio experience and one of my biggest bugbears is when audio geeks imply that audio has to be complicated. It doesn't. There's a lot of jargon out there and a lot of fear about the kind of technical ability, skill and equipment required. In truth, much of the process can be really simple - and cost-effective - if you start with the right equipment. In this book I will walk you through everything in order to get you started. I'll share the basics, how you can delve into more advanced audio production and what you need in order to outsource most of your podcast production if you wish to. Even if you plan not to do all of this yourself, you will have a basic understanding so that when you hit 'record' you'll know what to listen out for. I'll say it again: audio does not have to be complicated. If I can do this, so can you.

'I haven't got enough to say'

Are you worried that you don't have enough to say? That you'll create maybe six episodes and then wonder what on earth to follow them with? Well - if you know who your ideal client is, you also know what that listener needs to hear. You're aware of the problems they have, their pain points, the things they want in their life. (Don't worry - this book will walk you through the process of getting to grips with your perfect listener!)

By bringing in guests (if that's how you decide to run your show) it's not just what *you* have to say that matters. When you source guests with something valuable to share with your listeners, the onus is not all on you. All you need to know is what value you want to bring to your listeners - by ensuring your content answers and solves their problems, you'll never run out of material.

'There are too many people podcasting'

Everybody's jumping on the bandwagon. The market is too saturated. Hopefully, by reading this far you have seen the demographics and statistics I covered earlier. You'll have seen that this market is just getting going. That doesn't mean all you have to do is create a show and hope for the best. But it does mean that by creating good content you will ride this wave before everybody else jumps on board. You will still be an early adopter. Wait too long, and it'll be harder to make a splash. No one in business thinks it is a waste of time to start a blog, and yet there are over 610 million blogs online. No one thinks it is a waste of time to get on *YouTube*. Seriously, in comparison, hardly anyone is playing in this field. Yet.

'I don't have the right voice'

'I don't have the right voice for radio … I don't have the right voice for a podcast.' Well, you don't have to be perfect. It might reassure you to know that one of the reasons for podcasting's popularity is that we feel we get to know a podcast host. We like to hear the patterns of their voice. We like to hear when they stumble, when they stop and think. It makes us feel like we've got to know somebody better. Podcasting is not about perfection. It's about sharing your knowledge, your experience and the value you want to give to somebody else. It is first and foremost about communication. Many people will LOVE the quirkiness and unique timbre of your voice … but not if you don't press 'record'. In everyday life we're accustomed to hearing our own voice through the reverberation in our skull, so it can take a bit of getting used to hearing it recorded. Remind yourself that you have an important message to share, that it's time to put your fears and worries about being judged aside and get on with creating your podcast. Your work is more important than your fear. Besides, the rest of the world is used to hearing how you sound. Practise listening back. The more you hear yourself the easier it becomes to accept how your recorded voice sounds. Every voice is the right voice for podcasting. All you need to do is show up and be human.

'I don't have a big following'

Many aspiring podcasters think they don't have a big enough audience for a podcast to be worth their while yet. If you create your podcast strategically, do relevant research and have an effective launch plan, podcasting is one of the best ways to build your following. You will hit a much wider audience than by relying solely on *Facebook* or *LinkedIn* posts, live videos and using sales pages to build your email list. *YouTube* viewers are a different audience from podcast listeners. There is some crossover, but on the whole people are consuming podcasts because audio is their preferred method of obtaining material. Remember - you grow your following by being intentional about guesting on other people's podcasts and who you have as guests.

Podcasting is among the most efficient ways to grow your audience.

If you are in any doubt about when (or whether!) it is the right time to start your podcast, I hope you can see that now is the perfect time. It's exciting to give you insights into how to make your podcast not just any old podcast, but a podcast that launches powerfully and continues to have impact. There is a right - and a wrong - way to start and launch a podcast. Follow my advice and you'll have a chance of becoming an international, top-ranking podcaster like my clients with shows that have put them on the map, reaching listeners across the globe and helping them build their brands. Let's make sure you do learn to podcast *properly*.

Podcast Spotlight

Amy Rowlinson, *Focus on WHY*

Working with coaching clients and spending a lot of time on personal development, the idea of *Focus on WHY* came to me whilst sleeping! I woke up knowing that this new concept was what I needed to deliver and within a month I had launched the *Focus on WHY* podcast.

Focusing on the importance of WHY, I ask my guests to share their WHY - essentially what it is they do and why they do it - leading to relatable, uplifting and inspiring conversations with people from all walks of life. A simple concept yet with a powerful perspective!

Focus on WHY has now been live for just over three months. In that time 67 episodes have been released with over 100 recorded and more scheduled in the pipeline. It's been downloaded in 54 countries and currently features in *Apple Podcast Charts* in 16 countries across three categories with #4 being my highest position so far.

Even though I had a sound knowledge of podcasting, there was so much more that I didn't know and have since learned from Anna, particularly around monetization and the more technical aspects. *The Podcast Membership* and the *Podcast Membership Facebook* group have proven invaluable in terms of having Anna on hand to answer any of the questions I have had and to be able to connect with other podcasters. The checklists and step-by-step videos are simple to follow and easy to apply and as new content continues to be added into the *Membership* I am still in it five months later.

Without a comprehensive understanding of all the podcasting processes I am not sure I would have made such an impact from day one reaching #4 in the *Apple Podcast Entrepreneurship* charts. Anna's training has been invaluable and I am very grateful for her support and her time assisting me in getting this podcast off the ground and for it to be as much of a global success as it has been to date.

I have had people reach out to me from all over the world wanting to work with me and receive 1:1 coaching. Podcasting has helped me to establish at speed an incredible global reputation for my business and my personal brand making valuable connections with people in the process.

Go straight to Anna and talk to her about your plan for a podcast. She has carefully constructed *The Podcast Membership* to assist you through all the steps required. It's particularly important to go through the early stages of your podcast concept thoroughly to truly understand WHY you want to host a podcast,

WHO the audience is going to be, WHAT you are trying to deliver before launching into the HOW you actually do it. Anna covers all of these elements in her comprehensive training. It's a total no-brainer for any potential podcaster.

2

WHAT I WISH I HAD KNOWN ABOUT PODCASTING .... AND WHY YOU SHOULD LISTEN TO ME

I wrote this book because I was frustrated by the lack of decent books on podcasting. I found that they were either lead magnets to entice you to take an online course (nothing wrong with that if they provide good, useful and useable value) but flimsy in content, or they were written by people with decent-sized podcasts but lacking real audio knowledge and experience ... or audio experts without an effective podcast launch but whose understanding of the technology was advanced and therefore complex and over-complicated for the task at hand. I had a vague notion that I would eventually turn my entrepreneurial mind towards creating a podcast course and ordered a few books to take on my summer holiday. One arrived and I opened it whilst sitting in my parents' garden one hot August afternoon. It was written by someone respected and well-known in podcasting and it was the most disappointing book I had ever read. It annoyed me that someone with so little knowledge was making money by giving out shoddy, incomplete information. Why wasn't someone teaching people how to REALLY get started with podcasting, filling in the gaps to ensure they had a chance of success? And then the penny dropped. I could teach this standing on my head and was better placed to do so than anyone I had yet encountered in the online entrepreneurial space. This realization felt like coming home. In deciding to enter the mindset and personal development space as a leader a few years before, I believed I was leaving behind my experience in audio and voice recording work. Now I realized how in-demand my insights and knowledge were to help lift, inspire and motivate people around the world.

You might wonder what gives me the credibility to instruct others on how to create a podcast (and you *should* wonder - if you're going to learn anything that will enhance your business, make sure it's from someone who has attained more than a modicum of success in their field of expertise). I will take you through from where I started in audio to where I am now on my podcasting journey. I have a background as a voiceover artist and voice actor, culminating in nominations & awards for my work, including stepping out on the red carpets in Hollywood. My first voiceover job was in 2001 and I often did recording sessions in London studios, in and around my theatre auditions and performances. I liked the depth and resonance a microphone could give to my naturally high-pitched tones. Even when I had my first baby and paused acting for a while I would pop into studios to record documentaries for the BBC or video games whilst my husband waited outside with our newborn. It became tricky to juggle the studio work with a young child and so I stopped actively considering voice work.

It wasn't until five years later, after a complication in my third pregnancy, that I considered audio work again. I had been told to expect that I may never walk again. I won't go into detail here as that isn't what this book is about (it is covered in my first book *Get Visible: How to Have More Impact, Influence and Income*.) Out of the blue on the way to hospital, which was pretty much the only time I used to leave the house at that time, I received a phone call from a recording studio. Someone had found my old voiceover demo gathering dust on their shelves in its compact disk case (with an overly serious black and white image of me on the front) and wanted to book me in for a full day session. I said no. My father overheard and made me call them back - despite my protestations that I was in too much pain and discomfort.

That turned out to be one of the most fortuitous

days of my life. I got to the studio - carried in by my husband - and did my best with crutches rather than my wheelchair. It took a monumental amount of determination. At lunchtime when the director, producer and client left to get food, I remained in the studio with the engineer. He casually mentioned that he wished he'd known I was injured as, if I had a microphone, I could have recorded remotely. He told me that increasingly, as technology improved, many voice talents now recorded from their own studios at home.

And that's when the plan began to evolve. If I could never walk again, I could still perform with my voice worldwide. I could still work at home around the children and have a career I loved.

The only issue was that as a total technophobe I had no idea how to do it. What I did have, though, was oodles of time on my hands. I spent many hours laid up in bed researching all I could about recording from home, editing, software, microphones and how to create great quality audio. I sought out every single book, every single training that I could.

Within a couple of years I had a thriving business from home, recording inside what used to be my airing cupboard - now transformed into a professional recording booth - creating audio for companies such as *Coca Cola*, *Aardman Animation*, *BBC*, *Mothercare*, *Next* - pretty much any of the giant retailers. I recorded commercials, corporate narrations, training videos and lots of their phone systems..

Not only was I working with international leading brands but the positive focus shifted my energy. I recovered physically. My health improved, and I believe this happened because of the positivity voice work brought to my life – the opportunity to be heard across the world. I loved using my voice to earn money. I'd record whilst my toddler slept and build my recording empire when the children were tucked up at night.

Once my youngest started nursery school I began looking beyond the kind of commercial content I was regularly booked for and paused to consider exactly the type of work I wanted to create. For a performer it is a luxury to be so overly-booked that you have choice. I realized that I wanted to work on creative projects that required more of my skills as an actress. With that in mind I sought out voice acting gigs such as video games, audiobooks and radio dramas. I *niched down*. Within a few years of working committedly in those fields and seeking opportunities to become visible, I became an international multi-award-winning voice actor. I was a finalist multiple times in Hollywood for awards as an outstanding performer. On the whole, I produced most of the tens of thousands of hours of audio myself from within my home studio - my airing cupboard -

because it was the only place that would fit my wheelchair.

What I want you to understand is that I am not just somebody who has whacked up a few podcasts on *iTunes* and thinks I know enough to tell you how to do it. I'm someone with extensive learning and tangible experience within the audio industry. I created Hollywood-quality audio from home that has been used on movies, high-profile commercials, broadcast platforms including TV, radio and film around the world, and I have narrated and produced over one hundred audiobooks, many of which are international bestsellers. I've co-narrated with the best of the best in the audio industry, with voices that make up the background soundscape of your world.

There is a photograph of me on the red carpet in Los Angeles where I was a finalist for my seventh audio award, amongst the most incredible talent. It was on this night that I realized I wanted to enter the self-development arena, using my qualifications as a Master NLP Practitioner and experience of up-levelling my career. I wanted to help people spread their own message, get their own talents and skills seen and heard. I saw that my road from being disabled and not believing that I could achieve anything, to being here walking on the red carpet as an industry leader, enabled me to share something bigger with other talented, capable people not getting the results they want in their own business. Podcasting later became part of that journey. But at that moment, in that photograph, I thought I was leaving audio behind. I went into the business and mindset field to help people get visible. I was already coaching people from within that niche industry and I wanted to bring that work into many more entrepreneurial and creative people's lives. That whole journey for me is about *visibility* … and a key part of that is sharing your message, which, in turn, is what you do with a microphone, on camera and in your social media. I want you to understand that podcasting is becoming a vital tool in authority building.

As I've already said, podcasting is about to explode as an industry and you should be there from the beginning. Huge numbers of people are tuning in for the first time every day. And it is vital if you want to stand out from the crowd and be seen as one of the leading experts within your field. Podcasting allows you to spread your message internationally. It allows you to reach ears that you cannot reach via your social media content alone. Podcast listeners are loyal. They are also always looking for new, engaging content. When they find a great show, or a great episode, listeners are wonderful at sharing those episodes with their friends and colleagues.

I thought I was leaving my audio experience behind as I came into this entrepreneurial and coaching space. Then I heard, shortly after launching my online business, that a podcast could be a good way to bring in new clients and reach potential followers. However, it would likely take three years to gain any traction. I thought, why wait? Creating audio was a doddle for me, so I recorded and uploaded my first episode, and it was live within 48 hours. I was a podcaster.

At that time, *I did not know what I did not know*. I did no research beyond how to get my show onto *iTunes* and as embarrassing as this is, I hadn't even listened to a podcast or even worked out where the app was on my phone. And yet I was still a podcaster.

Hosting that first show taught me a lot, mostly from trying to work out why I didn't have many listeners. Audio quality was not the issue but pretty much every-thing else was! I would record an episode and tell no-one it was live. I didn't even announce that I had a show. I did have some loyal listeners and it eventually began to grow, but nothing impressive. Going back to basics made a big difference and my audience swelled. Clients began booking me directly for my coaching packages. Now my podcast was *worth* my time and effort. However, the more research I did, the more I understood that how a podcast is *launched* is vital in gaining solid traction. I'd missed that unique window of opportunity.

It appeared that podcasting had way more potential than I had anticipated and with a few tweaks my show began to gain momentum in terms of listener figures. I found more and more of my friends, family and peers were talking about podcasts they were listening to, recommending those they loved, and sharing shows that made them stop and think. I soon encountered other experienced podcasters who were using their shows to fuel their vast audiences. It was time to integrate everything I had uncovered.

At the same time, I was coming across business owners, coaches and entrepreneurs who were frustrated with not getting their message out to enough people. They were tired of posting content on social media for it to be pretty much lost after 24 hours. It dawned on me then how powerful podcasting is for creating long-term, long-lasting, far-reaching content. Where others in my field were floundering, I, and others who were already podcasting, were beginning to flourish. I came across more and more people who saw that a podcast could be a valuable asset in terms of positioning.

It was also evident that many people were struggling with how to make podcasting work. They would either shy away from the concept of podcasting at all or be crippled by fear of the technology required. I am passionate about making audio creation super simple and knew I could make a difference. I'd encounter new podcasters who would launch their podcast but had no idea about how to make it a profitable, valuable tool for business growth . It would just be something they did on the side that was kind of a loose cannon, and which quickly became a headache of a commitment. And I've done it that way too. I've also done it so that my podcast works very successfully to bring in leads for my business - and I know which way works better. I'm determined to share my early podcasting challenges and failings as well as my learnings and gains. I'm actually glad that I got it all wrong first time around because it makes what I teach much more useful and relevant to you.

You can podcast from anywhere. I've produced episodes while walking the dog, sitting in the car, giving a talk on stage. Sometimes I'll use my recording studio. Sometimes I'll record from my office. Even though most of your content should be of high-quality sound, many podcasts are created with a portable set-up. It's simply a matter of understanding the basics and taking the listeners on that journey with you. Recording at a conference? Tell the listener where you are and what's happening around you. Recording whilst out for a walk? Describe your experience. For the listeners, this is interesting. They feel part of your world. Understand that podcasting is an accessible medium that you can integrate and fear-mongering around technology is totally unnecessary. When I started out as a voiceover artist and was working for brands like *Coca Cola*, one of my peers said to me at the first industry event I went to: 'Well, you can't possibly start creating voice material unless you have a £10,000 recording studio.' I had a £25 microphone. You don't need expensive equipment. You *do* need good quality equipment, though, and I will take you through the kind of technology to be aware of and the kind of equipment to consider buying. And I promise to make it simple.

For those of you who do love your technology, I will go into a little more depth. Chiefly I want you to understand that a podcast can be straightforward and simple to create. There will always be options to upgrade and it's fine to invest heavily on your initial outlay if technology is something you love. Be reassured, though, that if you don't have that money or you're not interested in the technology, I'll show you exactly how you can get started with a minimum spend of around $100.

As an international speaker on the subject of audio, I've spoken at events in London, Chicago, New York and Hollywood about creating quality audio from home studio set-ups, how you can use your voice to improve the message you're putting out. I was part of a wave of early adopters of professional home studio use in the UK for international work and I was frequently invited onto panels to challenge outdated concepts that the microphones and recording set-ups were sub-par.

I now host two podcasts that are live on podcast directories. My current podcast is called *Entrepreneurs Get Visible*. When I launched this in October 2019 it was with real intent and purpose. I knew the audience I wanted to reach. I knew that I wanted this podcast to help position my first book, due to launch six weeks later. I knew I was ready to create podcast trainings for more entrepreneurs and business owners. I wasn't satisfied with teaching others how to podcast successfully when I didn't have the podcasting pedigree credentials to prove I knew what I was doing. I had to walk my walk and make sure that this podcast was successful. I set about putting into action all of my learning - gleaned from two years of experience - endless training and books on the subject, together with new-found knowledge on how to launch gained through being mentored by some of the UK's leading entrepreneurial figures, enabling me to create a six figure income from scratch in just over a year.

Within days of *Entrepreneurs Get Visible* being released it shot to #3 in the *iTunes* charts in the UK. It went to #9 in the charts globally in business categories within a week and for four weeks I was the only solo female host in the top 20. It later became an international #1 ranking podcast. As a result of that catapulting into the charts I was able to get my podcast into highly-coveted categories such as *New and Note-worthy* and *Top Shows* in *iTunes*. My podcast was promoted alongside, and then ahead of, Tony Robbins, Gary Vaynerchuk, Amy Porterfield and Marie Forleo - giants in the business and mindset fields with millions of followers each. I do not have their massive audiences (I'm working on it) but I had a successful podcast launch because everything about that show was created to be impactful.

The *iTunes* algorithms indicated that *Entrepreneurs Get Visible* was receiving many downloads, reviews and listens because of my focused efforts, and the platform began to promote the show for me. That is the power of a launch done properly. As a result of that visibility I could leverage much higher-profile, quality guests with little effort. This opened up my show to wider audiences. I could also now land myself as a guest on much more high-profile podcasts.

As I said, *Entrepreneurs Get Visible* podcast was created as part of an entire rebrand for my business in preparation for the launch of my first book. It was intended to be a vehicle for getting my book out there and read by as many people as possible. Bearing in mind that I self-published with no publishing knowledge, it did have the successful launch I wanted for it. It shot to #1 in 11 categories on *Amazon* and was in the top 10 in another nine categories for a period of time both in the UK, the US and several countries across Europe. As far as I'm concerned, this is because of the huge amount of downloads I get from my podcast every single day. In the first week or two after launch my book was bought predominantly by members of my podcast audience.

New podcasters began asking how I'd achieved these results and I realized I wanted to help as many as possible to get their shows out there. I created *The Podcast Membership*, full of online trainings, workbooks, videos and resources together with a community to support each other's launches. As I write this, every single member who has launched so far has achieved a top-ranking podcast position within the top ten in the *iTunes* charts, either in the UK or internationally. I have a blueprint that works … *if you work it*. Driven to share the potential of podcasting and bring established, aspiring and new podcasters together, I formed a free online *Facebook* group called *The Podcast Community*. I would love for you to join us and share your journey to a successful launch … and connect with others to find guests and be a guest yourself. You can find us on Facebook at: *www.facebook.com/groups/ThePodcastCommunity*. I am now CEO of a podcast production agency, with a fully 'done-for-you' service to take care of the editing, hosting and show notes creation for other podcasters and with a bespoke launch and monetize consultancy service which you can find at:

www.annaparkernaples.co.uk/podcast-production.

I hope you can see that I bring knowledge, passion, experience and support to the creation of audio. I bring entrepreneurial know-how about launching, growing and monetizing your podcast. Here, I'm making it as simple as possible for you to get your podcast out into the world. I want to take away those tech headaches, take away that fear that you don't know what you're doing. I want you to feel empowered. I want you to know that you have choices for upgrading your equipment when ready, or if interested. Podcasting can be simple and can integrate into your life seamlessly. I want you to know that you can make this a core part of your business. You won't be putting out 'just' some other content. You'll be producing something that can really matter to those who tune in and make a huge difference to the effectiveness of your business. Hopefully you can see and understand why this audio space is significant and how you can make it work for you.

I believe that as podcasters we are emerging, aspiring or established leaders. We have knowledge, experience and stories that can transform lives, finances, mental health, relationships, business results and self-respect. There are people with unusual hobbies who want to learn more and connect with others. There are people who need lifting, inspiring and entertaining. I want to create a ripple effect – my aim is to help you make a tiny change for one listener at a time.

Since I started running *The Podcast Membership* in early 2020, we've had many shows launch with impact and become international #1 podcasts, hitting the *US Top 100* charts and enabling the hosts to become leaders in their fields. I'm excited to help you do the same.

Podcast Spotlight

Kelly Forrester & Martin Miller, *Entrepreneur Truths*

We launched *Entrepreneur Truths* because we recognised the importance of REAL entrepreneurs having a space to share their stories - highs, lows and everything in between - to resonate, inspire and take our listeners Over The Edge.

We had purchased some of our equipment yet lacked the courage to start. We had no real idea how to put everything together to record, market and produce our podcast show. What Anna did was provide 24/7 access to powerful tools that guided us every step of the way. She revealed hugely important steps we would have failed to take and this would have undoubtedly resulted in poor impact and reach. We also enjoyed being part of a podcast community where we could ask for input into graphics and creation of our show. We used four of Anna's recommendations for artwork, music, hosting and website hosting. I've recommended Anna to absolutely EVERYONE. We can't praise or recommend Anna enough – seriously, she's ahead of all the other podcast gurus who claim to be this ... or that... Anna is the real deal! No surprise she's crowned the Podcast Queen!

Without Anna's help we would have failed to work as fast and smart. Visibility would have been hugely decreased and we may have lacked the confidence to do it.

The impact of podcasting on our business has been HUGE!!!! Seriously, the calibre of guests we are securing for our show is WORLD CLASS because we have produced an extraordinary show! We have secured new business and are seen as advocates of REAL entrepreneurs as a global training and development company. This is extremely POWERFUL. We have received incredible feedback from our guests and listeners who all say our interview technique and interviews are like nothing else!

We featured in *New & Noteworthy*, *Top Shows on Apple* and specifically under *Business Top Shows, New Shows & Entrepreneurship* on *Apple*. We reached #8 in *UK Apple Podcast Business Category*. We are now positioned globally in 15 countries. Peak position so far has been #338 *Global Chartable* business category.

If you're considering producing a podcast show, it can be as light touch or intense as you want it to be. Either way, Anna's expert guidance is world class and will put you on the path to take action! What are you waiting for?!

3

HOW TO PLAN YOUR PODCAST FOR MAXIMUM IMPACT

Hosting your own podcast is a badge of honour. Most people in your industry won't get around to doing it, so your comparative credibility and authority will increase. Yet, that badge alone is not enough to make your podcast successful. A podcast with very few listeners will quickly feel like a waste of time and an atrophied opportunity, and I'm sure that isn't what you want. The planning stage is crucial to ensure that your podcast gets a head start in striking a chord. I'll openly admit I didn't spend enough time (or indeed any!) on this stage when I launched my first podcast. If I had, I'd have had much better results in the first six months, and much more growth and all-round impact. Don't do what I did. Do what I wish I had done, now with hind-sight, experience and greater knowledge about podcasting behind me. The reason my second podcast was so successful is that I gave the planning stages attention.

Putting out regular unscripted content inevitably means that your listeners will get to know a fair bit about you. Before you worry about oversharing, remember how useful sharing your own quirks, preferences and foibles can be. As listeners we enjoy that intimate, behind-the-scenes peek into someone's life and business. We love to feel as though we KNOW someone. That's what a great podcast allows. When we like and know someone, we instinctively trust them and where there is trust, there is a much easier sale somewhere down the line.

What will your podcast lead people towards? What are the primary and secondary aims of your show? To establish you as an expert? To build community? Is it an extended invitation for prospective clients and customers to join your mailing list? Is it about industry kudos and standing out from the crowd? Whatever it is, you're in luck. A fully prepared podcast can achieve all of these.

There are many podcasts a listener could pick from - even in your tiny, minuscule, niche field - so being clear about the purpose of your podcast is paramount to its success. Clarity enables your listener to decide who to listen to (we'll look at establishing your *perfect listener* in greater detail in the next chapter). Does it say 'on the tin' (ok ...actually, the *iTunes* description) what your podcast is about, who it is for and what they can learn? Is it easy to understand why listening would be of benefit - not just to you, your mum and your best friend, but to someone who has never encountered you before? One of the wonders of podcasting is that you can be found by people who would never usually come across you anywhere else, and from far flung corners of the world.

Let's spend a moment getting a few insights into what you hope to achieve by becoming a podcaster:

The reason I wish to start podcasting is ...

I've heard that podcasting can be ...

As a result of my podcast, financially I'd like to be able to ...

Podcasting will also give me ....

I will know my podcast has been successful when ....

My biggest hope for my podcast is ....

Through my podcast, I would like to help others to achieve the following ...

The purpose of my podcast is to ...

This supports my business in the following ways ...

By sharing my message with the world, I will achieve the following change ...

In case you hadn't already guessed, the impact of

running a podcast is the bit that makes me tick. You can reach so many people, hitherto unknown to you, and touch their lives (and businesses) in an intimate way. But, as I said before, you can't help everyone - it just does not work. Stop and think whom exactly you wish to impact.

Planning is the most crucial part of getting your podcast together. It will help you understand who you're creating it for, what you want it to do for your business and everything else that is going to drive more impact towards the message. Before you rush in, think long and hard about this. What are you interested in talking about? What do you feel you are sufficiently passionate about that you can discuss with ease, with flow, without having to overthink, without having to overcomplicate? What do you love talking about? If you're not passionate about your topic, it will come across in your voice, your tone, your energy and the non-verbal ways listeners pick up on communication nuances. Where does your passion lie? Because yes, right now you want to start a podcast. What about when you've been doing it for a year? Or two or three? What about when you've been doing this for five years? Podcasts can take a while to grow and build those audiences. Make sure from the start that this is something you really are genuinely interested in.

What is your passion?

What do people ask you for advice on? What do you talk about with friends, peers, colleagues? What do you have expertise in? It might be that you're at the beginning of a new venture or changed fields recently. Whatever, there is an area you wish to carve your mark on, to become known as an expert in, even if you are initially facilitating conversations with other people rather than leading the expertise. Your podcast will show people that this is a topic you are *invested* in. Whatever your topic, this is where those two areas - your passion and your expertise – meet … where the easiest, most enjoyable content for your podcast will be found. I urge you again: review your topic of authority *before* you begin hosting.

When launching my first podcast, initially named *Inspiring Mummy Club*, I didn't pause to evaluate if I wanted to be known as the person talking about being a mummy long-term. Is that really who I am and what excites me? Within months I admitted to myself that this was not an area I wanted to pigeon-hole myself into. My message was for ambitious individuals, already on a path to attaining success, already running businesses. I felt disconnected from listeners who wanted to reach out about how challenging being a mum can be and how to juggle childcare, how to cope with their babies and toddlers. The growth of my business and podcast led to renaming the show *Inspiring Success Podcast* and later to the launch of my second podcast *Entrepreneurs Get Visible*. These evolutions came about because I was more motivated, aligned and interested in talking to people who are ready to accelerate and create exceptional results.

I am genuinely engaged with and excited about everything I've created with my second podcast. And I'm enthusiastic to learn and share the content. My podcast content is no longer all about the children at home, it's about getting out into the heart of your industry and getting the results you want. This makes me tick and I have found my flow. Do not create your podcast on a whim. Stop to think about what you want to be seen, heard and remembered for.

The purpose of your podcast

What is the purpose of your podcast?

How will your show serve you, your business and your listeners?

How will you generate income growth and business leads as a result of your podcast?

Where are you driving people towards with your show (something I'll be discussing in more depth later)?

I don't want you to create a podcast and be excited

about it for the first few months, only to feel a kind of heaviness because you don't know what to do with it from thereon. I want you to see your show as being of core value to your business - an efficient, quirky way for people to come into your world, your business funnel, your email list … to buy your products, to buy your service, to create awesome jaw-dropping possibilities for you. That is the potential power of podcasting.

It's important to say at this point, though, that these results are not automatic. I won't pretend that it is instantly achievable to increase your income and influence through podcasting. It takes work, consistency and determination.

Consider - what do you want your podcast to achieve for you and your brand? For your income? Or is there a stronger community element that you want to bring together? Maybe there's a real need or drive that you have to serve, that is beyond the selling, beyond the revenue, and is much more about bringing a niche part of an industry or community together. Is your podcast about collaboration? Think about who you want to associate with, to connect with and be positioned alongside within your field. Have clarity about these elements right from the start as it will inform all of your decisions.

People listen to podcasts because they want to be educated, entertained and connected. How does that fit with your business model and what you can provide? For what purpose will your listeners join you week in, week out? What will they take away from your show? What do they hope for when they tune in? To what extent will you fulfil that hope? What feeling of belonging will they have? Understanding insights like these early on will make a huge difference to your show's initial and ongoing success.

Again, we'll cover the *perfect listener* in greater detail later, but with everything you create, always consider who the podcast is actually for. Newsflash! Your podcast is not just about *you*, even if you're using it as a brand-building or authority piece. Decide who it is for and how it will serve them and their needs.

Show format

Let's have a look now at the kinds of episodes you could create. The beauty of podcasting is that there are no hard and fast rules. In principle, you can create your podcast any way you want. In practice, it is worth considering the best format to share your knowledge and have conversations that matter.

Solo Show

There are pros and cons to a solo show. You're not reliant on anybody booking into your diary ... you don't have to research and reach out to connect with guests. You don't have to worry about someone else's audio quality. You just have your knowledge, the microphone and your own schedule. You can create podcast episodes whenever you please. There is considerable freedom and flexibility in this set-up style. The downside is that you don't have anyone to bounce ideas off. The content is dependent on you, your insights and experience. And when you are in flow, a solo show is easy to create ... but what about those days when you simply aren't in the mood to record? Or when personal matters take over? Your listeners still expect to hear from you. And without guests, you don't have the same opportunities to benefit from other people's audiences and followers.

So what about a mix? I currently create two episodes a week – one is a guest interview and one is a shorter solo show. I can make best use of my own expertise and thoughts and also have interesting conversations with guests. It may be that alternating styles is an option for you.

Interviews

One of the most popular show styles is the interview format. This is perhaps the easiest to create and gives you opportunities to grow your listenership as your guest will most likely promote the episode to their own audience (there is a section on how to get the most out of interviews later in this book). On the upside, you only have to do basic research and planning as the best interviews are natural in conversation. The downside is constantly having to source new guests and mutually convenient times to record. I've loved many of the interviews I've done, and this was how my first podcast started. It has opened me and my work up to bigger audiences and has helped to build strong connections with other entrepreneurial leaders. I have in-depth, intimate conversations that bring me joy, personal connection and purpose.

With any interview show, think about how your guests will be of benefit to you, to build your profile and connections and get you in front of a larger network ... whilst at the same time providing value to your audience. One of my mistakes with that first podcast was to bring on a guest and then label the episode with the guest's name only. For listeners and search engine optimization (SEO), that title gave no clue as to why they should listen. This is especially true with guests who don't yet have an established following. Even if you are fortunate enough to have high-profile guests, the value, content, takeaway, education and learning from that show need to be clear from the outset.

Something else to consider is hosting a show where you are completing a physical activity with your guest whilst speaking with them. Your job here is to paint a visual of what's going on whilst you hold a conversation. This can be challenging from an audio perspective, although lots of fun for your listeners. It would work well for a podcast around sport, creative pursuits or cooking, for example. I've listened to a show about how women feel about their bodies, throughout which the co-hosts and guest removed their clothes. They described what they were wearing and why, and revealed how they felt about undressing. They painted a verbal picture of their naked bodies for the listener. It is at once vulnerable and engaging. As a listener, you are privy to the emotional and physical experience. If you decide to do similar (not necessarily in the buff!) you cannot be too detailed with description. Finding the balance between conversation flow and description is a challenge but can make for entertaining content.

Co-hosting

If you're thinking of co-hosting, consider if you will each take responsibility for leading alternate shows or if you will always host together. It takes a little while to build those on-mic relationships, to know when to interrupt and when to sit back and let the other host lead. It takes increased co-ordination to sync your diaries and plan your episodes. Will you do it remotely or will you be in the same room? What will happen if one of you is unwell? Who owns the intellectual property? How will you future-proof for what happens when your working relationship comes to an end, even if that seems impossible or unlikely? My advice would be to submit your show into *Apple Podcasts* under a business-specific email address rather than a personal *iTunes* account, as it will not be possible to transfer at a later date. Co-hosting can be a great deal of fun, however it's important to protect both parties from the worst possible eventual outcome should relationships break down. I've seen several co-hosted shows come to an abrupt end and it's a pity that these issues were not ironed out at the planning stage. Whatever decisions you make, get them down in writing with signatures from both parties. Trust me, you'll be glad you actioned this advice.

Round Table

This is self-explanatory. A number of people sit around a table, perhaps even using a single microphone, and discuss a given subject. More than four people becomes challenging to manage and to ensure each person gets a chance to speak, although it can be an enjoyable way to bring content to your listeners. Remember to introduce each voice early on in so that the listener can follow who is who. There are no set rules beyond ensuring you don't talk over each other too much - uncomfortable for the listener experience and a challenge in the editing suite. You may want some non-verbal cues to indicate who wants to interject next and you may want to nominate one individual to chair the conversation.

Length of episodes

Decide how long you would like each episode to be. Whilst there are no industry standards or guidelines, podcasts tend to range from 10 minutes to just under an hour. When and where is your content likely to be consumed by your listeners? What snippets of time do they want to fill? Choose an approximate length and stick to it in the first few months of your podcast hosting. It'll give listeners some degree of comfort knowing that they can listen to a particular length episode at a certain time and incorporate your show into a routine.

Frequency of episodes

The same goes for the regularity with which you release your podcast. Routine appeals to people on both sides of the podcasting experience - hosts and listeners. Plan to schedule an episode to release at the same time every week, fortnight or even day to give fans the best chance of tuning in. This will increase your opportunities for downloads. Make sure that the amount you commit to is sustainable - not overwhelming - and will still afford you ample opportunity to grow your audience. If you're hoping to make it to *iTunes Top Show* lists, they definitely favour regular content over sporadic releases.

Audio vs Video

Whilst the majority of podcasts are audio-only there are some that include video content. Before you choose the medium for your show consider your audience's needs. Maybe run a poll in the online communities you are part of to see if there is content preference. One of the reasons podcasts are popular is that it is primarily a hands-free, eyes-free consumer scenario. You can upload video-only podcasts in most hosting platforms in the same way as you would an audio-only show, but the editing requirements will take longer. One way to create content for both video and audio lovers is to video your interviews and upload them to *YouTube* or similar, then upload the audio to your podcast host. This book focuses primarily on audio podcasts, but the concepts from planning to launch are the same and there are benefits from a SEO perspective of putting your show on *YouTube*.

Live Shows

Podcasts with a 'live show' element are gaining popularity, with listeners witnessing a podcast show recording. Whilst you may not begin this way you could monetize your show down the line by hosting exclusive live broadcast events. And instead of physical attendance, it could be 'live' via online streaming where people ask you questions remotely in real-time. An exclusive event is something to consider for special one-off episodes - perhaps when you reach your 50th or your 100th - or something to build into the structure of your show from conception. It can be a lucrative addition to your podcast monetization repertoire.

It all comes down to the purpose of your podcast. For my current show the first 30 episodes were solo -

short, sweet and to the point. That was deliberate and enabled me to release daily episodes for 30 days straight in order to build momentum quite quickly. The intention was to switch to interviews only, to bring on influential guests within the coaching and entrepreneurial space on a weekly basis. However, the short, punchy episodes were popular with my listeners and I realized that if I let that element go - and the positive feedback I was getting - I'd be missing a trick and not serving my audience to the best of my ability. People were saying they found the faster, energetic pace of my delivery refreshing and motivating. I knew also that I wanted to conduct interviews in order to grow my network, show reach and personal brand. To compromise I released a combination of content: an interview on Mondays and a short, to the point episode with my own personal stamp on it on Thursdays - my own energy, learnings and experiences. I may change this this over time, and if I do, I will communicate any changes with my audience so that they feel part of the process.

If you're podcasting to build a loyal tribe (and believe me - if you get your podcast right, you will achieve that with quality content) with fans expecting a daily or weekly show and suddenly disappear for a few weeks before coming back and doing three shows at once, you're going to lose that hard-won trust factor.

Again – return to the purpose of your podcast. What are you helping people with? How often will they want that content? Daily? Weekly? Twice weekly? Monthly? Fortnightly? How will you make podcasting fit with your current business commitments? How much time and attention can you give to podcasting so that it doesn't become an onerous task? I recommend carving out regular slots of non-negotiable weekly time in your calendar to focus on your podcast, not just for recording but to plan guests and reflect on the lessons you want to share with your audience.

Episodic vs Series.

There is also the option of using a serial format as well as episodic releases. If you are short on time or concerned about the amount of valuable content you can create, this could be the solution. You could create a series of six, 10 or 12 episodes on one topic, leaving the show live and never releasing any further series, or you could 'go dark' for a few months or even a year and then release a second (or third series). The positive side of this is that there is less pressure to maintain a recording schedule whilst continuing to use the podcasting arena to establish your expertise. When releasing a new series you can effectively re-launch the entire show, giving you more potential for reaching a new audience for a short time. The downside is that if people enjoy your podcast they'll want to listen to content of a similar vein. Undoubtedly your competitors will have podcasts that serve their demands, leaving you at risk of losing your momentum and loyal listenership.

Batch recording

I will admit that there were times with my first show when I fell behind with getting the content recorded and scheduled. With the best will in the world, life happened and I found I was having to create episodes on the fly. It became quite a pressure. I urge you to create a podcasting routine that fits with the rest of your life and business commitments. I tend to record most of my content in batches on one day of the month. I'll plan interviews for that day and batch record solo episodes. I currently outsource most of the production elements of my podcast, the perks of running a podcast production agency - I can record and upload whilst the rest is taken care of (although I did everything from editing to promotion for the first two years of podcasting). I upload the recordings to a *Dropbox* folder and communicate with my editor and VA (Virtual Assistant). I look over the schedule of releases and the dates where no guests are booked in for future recordings. I know that we will either have a number of potential guests to approach or that we may need to sift through guest applications. One thing you'll find as a podcast host is that you'll suddenly become popular. I receive emails on an almost daily basis with requests to come on my show (we'll cover why most of these receive a 'no' later in this book). By batch recording I can give my show attention and focus and then move on to other business tasks for the rest of the month. I look forward to that day of recording and connecting. On a weekly basis I review what needs to happen in terms of show promotion.

I would recommend that you allocate at least an hour a day to your podcast until you launch. From then, I recommend at least one day a month for focusing on it - getting it all scheduled and batched. This way your podcast will become an integral, easy part of your business. Be honest with how much time you have for it – you don't want to get somewhere down the line, maybe three, six or eight months after launch, and find you're not as passionate about it anymore. When you commit to your schedule, you'll need to know you'll maintain that commitment.

Hopefully this chapter has given you some firmer ideas on how to run your show. In the coming chapter, you will understand who you want to be heard by.

Podcast Spotlight

Susana & Oliver Silverhøj, Pam Lob, *Live the Impossible Show*

Less than 27 hours after our launch of *Live the Impossible Show* we reached international #1 on *Apple* podcast charts. Within a week we were on the charts in seven different countries and on the "new and noteworthy podcast" chart in UK.

The support of Anna Parker-Naples has been the key to our success. Anna's deep knowledge and understanding - that comes together in her step-by-step process and personal support in *The Podcast Membership* - has made the possibly overwhelming process of creating an impactful podcast easy and joyful. We went from a spontaneous idea of creating a podcast to an amazing product we are super proud of in a couple of months and we have enjoyed every step of the way. Who knew that could even be possible? We can really recommend Anna's work and feel very blessed to have worked with her.

If we had not had Anna's help we would

have given up from the overwhelm of all the different aspects to consider and do before you launch a podcast. However, podcasting has increased our reach and audience and provided some amazing collaborations and new products we didn't even think of before.

Our advice for anybody thinking about starting a podcast is look into your WHY. Why would you like to do a podcast? Do it if you enjoy communicating with likeminded, inspiring people, if you want to get visible and have structure in your business. If you like to wing it in your business as a hobbyist or if you are looking for a quick fix to make loads of money, podcasting is maybe not the best medium. It takes courage, consistency and passion to make a difference. For us, podcasting is so much fun, feels free as well as meaningful - we just love it!

4

THE PERFECT LISTENER

If you've spent time online in entrepreneurial spaces or business coaching networks you'll know the benefit of working out your *ideal client avatar* for promoting and selling your services and products. The same is true of your podcast. Being specific about your perfect listener enables you to niche down in the words you use in all elements of your show - the title, the description, the episode titles, the show notes. It also helps with marketing - you have a greater appreciation of the pain or problem your potential clients are struggling with. These issues, fears and frustrations can be addressed in detail in your podcast, making your content valuable.

The next section delves into exactly who your perfect listener is. Even if you've done a lot of work ascertaining who you market your services to, it is well worth doing again for your listener. Our businesses shift and grow, as do our interests. If you're going to create hours of podcast episodes over the coming years it would pay to ensure you'll be enjoying speaking to the right people. When I started my first podcast, my business (and therefore podcast) was entirely focused on inspiring mums to take action to improve their mindset. Eight months into running my podcast it dawned on me that I no longer felt engaged with this audience. I didn't want to talk about sleepless nights and juggling the children. I didn't want to talk about self-care. Sure, as a mum, those topics naturally crop up in my content from time to time, but the struggle of motherhood is not a focus that lights me up. I have a different mission - to get people with an ambitious entrepreneurial bent to take massive action and get results. I ended up rebranding my podcast. Had I stopped to work out what I'm sharing with you in the following exercise, I wouldn't have wasted time building the wrong audience in the first place. Do yourself a favour and make sure that the content you're about to create is actually for people you want to serve. If there's even the slightest chance that your interest in the subject will dwindle after a few months, then re-think it now.

First and foremost, be clear on your target audience. Know exactly who you want to speak to and why your content matters to them. I'm not talking about a vague demographic such as 'Female, aged 28-45, married with kids'. That's a pretty broad category. Be precise about who you are addressing and the issues they are encountering and you'll get much better results. It'll be easier for prospective listeners to know, when they come across your show title in *iTunes*, that it is right for them. Your title and description will speak directly to them and their immediate needs. Take the demographic I've mentioned above: there's a big difference between the ages of 28 and 45. There's a world of difference between having small children and older teenagers or young adults who have left home. There's a long way from being in the first year of marriage to heading towards twenty years of marriage. In both scenarios, the 'aged 28-45, married with kids' fits. You get the point. Thinking about your ideal listener as a specific person will improve the listener's rapport with you.

Look at these examples:

Rosie is female, 32, married for 18 months with two children aged 12 months and five years respectively. She has a strong desire to not return to the corporate world in which she enjoyed her work at an executive level but felt undervalued over the two years since having her first child. After struggling with post-natal depression and juggling work/home life balance she is determined not to fall into that trap again.

Kelly is female, 43, married and on the verge of separation with two children aged 16 and 14. She has been running her retail business for 12 years with investment from other family members. She is ready to go into the online coaching space within the next 18 months.

The content you create for Rosie is different from the content you would create for Kelly, and a common concern is that by creating content aimed at Rosie you are alienating Kelly. This isn't true. Instead, it sharpens your output, and those who are intended for the message you share know instinctively that you are speaking to them and their challenges. You create much more of a sense of belonging and connection. By speaking to everyone, your material becomes generic and the power of your message becomes diluted.

Ask yourself these questions:

What problem can I help with?

Who has this problem?

How big is the problem for that listener?

Why is it important to talk about this subject?

How many people face this problem?

Does this problem affect different types of people?

How can I know for sure that these problems exist? Do I need to test my assumptions?

What *Facebook* groups could I visit to find out if my beliefs are true?

What research do I need to do?

What is the pain of the problem that I will help solve through my business?

What feelings are there about this problem?

What outcome do listeners want?

What desire do I want to help them fulfil?

What feelings can I help them to have?

What do my perfect listeners have in common? (Gender, age, marital status, children, income, country, religion, background, occupation, beliefs, etc.) Give as much detail as possible.

What is the problem in its simplest form?

How big is this pain point for my perfect listener?

Is my podcast a pain reliever or a gain creator? Or both?

What pain will I take away from my listeners' lives?

What will they be able to do as a result of my advice on the show?

What are their behaviours?

How can I reach them? Where do they hang out on social media?

What type of relationship do they want?

When building your podcast, do so with the listener in mind for absolutely everything. This includes the style of the show - upbeat or relaxed - content, show length, type of episode – short and snappy or longer and more relaxed - daily, monthly or weekly; how often the perfect listener will want your content. This will inform your branding - not just the artwork but also the style of the show - intros, outros, music, voiceover, all of the content that you create. Every episode that goes out should have your perfect listener in mind. Think about what they need to hear, learn and want to be educated on.

So - let's get down to the *perfect listener avatar.*

Before you go any further with your podcast, determine who your perfect listener is. What do they want to learn? How pushed for time are they? We're all super busy ... they'd probably love to sit down and read lots of books on their area of interest but don't have the time. They may not have the time to watch *YouTube* videos, or they may not have a preference for video material as a learning style. But with a podcast they have the option to consume content as they're going about their daily lives - and this is crucial.

Where does your listener want to belong? What kind of community and connection do they seek? Is there an industry they want to become established in? A skill they want to master? Understanding these motivations is key to knowing what you're going to build with your podcast. A podcast isn't just information or learning – it is a powerful way to build your own tribe … to build a community of like-minded individuals.

The more detail you can sketch out about a listener's life makes content creation easier. What does a typical day in their life look like? Where do they wake up? Who are they with? How much time do they have to get ready? What's their morning routine? Do they have to rush to catch a train, run to the bus stop? Do they have to take their children to school? What pockets of time do they have? When do they go to bed? What do they eat? Do they have a coffee break at work? Do they have a lunch break? How do they fill those segments of time? If they're commuting, are they working away from home? How long is the commute? What time do they return home? What happens in their world when they get through the front door? What responsibilities do they have and to whom?

Understanding what their everyday looks like will help you decide on the length of episodes to create. My audience for *Entrepreneurs Get Visible* tends to be time poor … they want information quickly and this informs my podcast style. One of my solo episodes is between 10 and 15 minutes long and I provide the information without much preamble. What style would suit your avatar? Will they want to consume lots of information in one go to learn a particular topic in all its depth or will they want something drip fed over a number of weeks? This will help you choose between creating specific series and ongoing episodes.

Knowing your perfect listener will help with choosing the perfect show name. This is covered fully in Chapter 5 on *Branding*, but your show title needs to appeal ... your listener should know straightaway what they're getting when they see your show advertised, when it crops up in *iTunes*, *Spotify*, *Google and* browser bars. Ambiguity is not your friend.

Your individual episode titles are key to building further traction with your perfect listener. The title must make it clear that the content is of value and that they should stay and listen. Every single episode title that goes out into *Podcast Land* becomes SEO-optimized. They are vitally important for brand-building and for establishing you as an authority in your industry. It is the same for your artwork and your audio branding. The colours should *speak* to the listener ... the fonts should not only be legible (see *Branding*) but communicate clearly that your podcast does what it says on the tin.

Reflect on their aspirations, ambitions and frustration with where they are in life. How far along the path to having a successful business or lifestyle are they? And - hugely informative as to how much time they have for themselves to build a new business, follow a dream, be listening to audio, where – on that journey - are they with their relationship status?

How will they listen? With headphones to prevent the sound spreading into someone else's personal space? Do they have a commute? The school run? Train, tube, car or bus journey? The length of those journeys informs the length of your episodes.

Do they look out for your episode every week? Will you create sufficient content to satisfy their hunger? When do they listen? Morning? Lunchtime? In the evening just before bed? This will inform the style, pace and delivery of your podcasts. What do they do when they listen? Many people listen as they exercise or do household chores. Some even listen in the shower.

I tend to do most of my listening as I'm doing household chores - when my attention is not elsewhere. I don't have a long commute so my podcast listening happens through earbuds as I potter around tidying the house and putting the washing on. When do you listen? If you don't yet listen regularly to podcasts, I urge you to start. It will give you a fuller appreciation of what you're creating and the benefits of the auditory experience.

After you've worked out how to grab the attention of your perfect listener, consider what might make them stop listening. Have they run out of time? Have they taken what they need to learn? Have they become bored or disengaged, or feel they have to wait too long to get to the point of the show? It's rare that I have time to listen to a podcast episode over 45 minutes long. I might think: 'Well, I've listened to most of that. I'll start with a fresh episode next time.' The numbers in Chapter 1 show that people tend to listen to about 80% of an episode. What should you include in the early sections of your episode in order to make people stay?

People starting a new venture or in the throes of a new passion or interest are potentially listening to podcasts because they want that connection with others who share those interests. Perhaps they don't have that support or guidance elsewhere. You and your podcast may well be the first to point them down the path to what they want to learn.

The perfect listener avatar is powerful because when you are clear on this, your listenership will grow organically. Your podcast will speak directly to them and directly to their problems. How big are those issues for your listeners? How urgent is that need to consume your information, to be part of the community, to learn and grow and educate themselves? How much do they want to change their current situation?

How do these individuals feel about the problem you'll talk about in your podcast? Frustrated? Embarrassed? Irritated? That emotional connection will inform the style of interview, the type of guests you bring on and the way you tackle the topic that you are an expert, or positioning yourself as an expert, in. What outcome do they want? What do they hope to feel when they've listened? When they've consumed all of your content? What do they hope to walk away with? This is really important - not only will you service their pain by removing that problem, you are also helping to create a gain for them. Your podcast may be the route to inspiration, motivation, action and recovery.

Make your perfect listener human. Be specific. Don't just say, 'Oh, it's a woman between 40 and 60 … she runs her own business.' That's too broad. Create somebody with a specific gender, age and marital status … children, no children; income, country, religious belief, education levels, occupation, values. Think about them as one person. I promise this will make it easier to engage in an ongoing one-sided conversation if you know who you're speaking to.

Make your avatar Kirsty, not Harriet. Kirsty is 34. She has three children and walks the dog twice a day. She has a partner but he's never home so she doesn't get much time to herself. She knows she has way more earning potential than her husband but isn't in a position to go after it whilst the children are small. She's not Harriet. Harriet is 58 and has a full-time job where she's been a senior leader for 15 years. She's divorced and lives on her own. She has lots of friends who are also senior leaders, and she knows nobody who is breaking out into running their own business. Kirsty and Harriet might well fall into a similar age bracket but their lives, immediate interests, wants and needs are significantly different.

Think about creating a podcast for Dave and not for Brian. Dave is a lover of motorbikes and every working day he dreams about where to go on his motorbike at the weekend. He knows that his job doesn't serve him beyond putting money in the bank and food on the table. What he really wants to do is to specialize in an industry connected with the biking that he loves. He turns to podcasts to gather as much information as he can to learn how to do that, whilst still doing a job he tolerates.

Brian, however, is a self-made multi-millionaire entrepreneur. He has a team of people to whom he outsources and delegates. Most of his personal life is spent sailing and spending time with his family on luxury holidays. The same podcast is unlikely to appeal to both men, yet both have entrepreneurial minds. I cannot stress enough the importance of variance in the specificity of your episodes, informing the quality of your content and ultimately the success of your podcast. Give your listener a name. An age. A specific location. Give them a background and a personal history. Type this out and print it up ... maybe even draw a picture of your avatar. The more personality you can imbue them with, the easier it is for you to speak to them.

Consider how you can dominate a particular area within podcasting. I have seen podcasts that focus on a specific style of crocheting become hugely popular. These shows speak to the listeners because they – the listeners – are not like everybody else. How can you service a niche interest with your content? I know this can be a bit scary to start with, but the more particular you are the better you can build a community of fans, allowing you to serve them in a richer way for their unique needs. The key to a successful podcast is to create fans, people who keep coming back to your material because they genuinely love it and feel a valued part of the show.

As you build your podcast, you are building a community, potentially with the option to create a thriving *Facebook* group or convert your listeners into paying clients who attend online or live in-person events, conferences or podcast recordings. You are establishing a sense of connection and belonging - a fundamental human need. It's what we all want - to feel that we belong, that we are part of a tribe of like-minded individuals. Bear that in mind whilst you create your show.

A podcast can make listeners feel, particularly in solo-style episodes, that you are addressing them personally. The strongest content in the marketplace plays on this intimacy. Yes, your episodes may be heard by thousands – not all together, but one single person at a time - in their car, on their commute, in their home.

Once your perfect listener profile is complete, put yourself in their shoes and consider what you would type into Google to solve your problems. This will give you valuable ideas for keywords to include in your podcast name, show description and individual episodes. Podcast directories such as *iTunes* work in a similar vein to standard SEO methods. Finding and utilizing the most effective terms connected with your perfect listener and their concerns will make a difference to your show's success. Inside *The Podcast Membership* we provide up-to-date recommendations for how best to achieve this. To get started, however, visit *ListenNotes.com* and *Google Trends* to begin your research.

Podcast Spotlight

Catherine Morgan, *In Her Financial Shoes*

I started my podcast to help empower women to be financially resilient … to bring a no jargon disruptive approach to the profession focusing on both the practical and emotional side of money.

I've since had 45k downloads, got to #3 in the investing charts on launch and #7 on launch of series 4 in January 2020 (the only female financial adviser in the UK top 10 charts). The podcast has also helped me to build an audience of raving fans with weekly transformational emails and reviews of how it's helped them to transform their relationship with money. My podcast has also led to features in *Readers Digest, The Times and Good Housekeeping.*

Anna helped me put together a launch strategy for a new series in 2020. She helped me drive a huge focus on download numbers and subscribers to the podcast. I went from 2200 average downloads per month in December 2019 to 8000 in one month

(January 2020). Without Anna I would have continued plodding along at a few thousand downloads per month

Podcasting has given me huge visibility in my profession, helping me stand out and be heard! It's also helped me connect with some fascinating influencers and guests which has led to other opportunities in my personal and business life. Podcasting is the future of content marketing. It is an incredibly exciting opportunity to be heard, to create impact by giving you a platform to share your knowledge and build connection with your tribe. It's also a great way to produce content that can be repurposed to grow assets in your business (content is one of the best assets for income and impact). If fear is holding you back from getting visible, podcasting is perfect. You don't even have to show your face and it can be edited! So what are you waiting for?!

5

BRANDING YOUR PODCAST

The presentation and packaging of your podcast has the potential to attract listeners and conversely switch them off before they even hit play. The name, colours, design, artwork, fonts and layout help them to decide instinctively to listen or to overlook. If your podcast makes it through, the next step the potential listener encounters is the show description. If that appeals, they may make it as far as to hear the first few seconds of your show - where they encounter your intro - a professional voiceover, or your own voice, with or without music. Split second judgements are made regarding quality, and each of these hurdles must be crossed before the listener even hears the beginning section of your episode. Careful planning is vital for your show to have the best chance of capturing (and retaining) attention.

Naming Your Show

The most important thing about your podcast's title is that it is clear to the listener what the content is about and why they should listen. Communicate through the title that this podcast is for them. The name should excite or intrigue them and elicit an emotional response. It's tempting to brand your show with a creative or clever name, and that's fine, particularly if it's part of your already established brand. However, if what people will get and why they should click on your show's image in the first place is unclear it will be harder for you to gain traction. Given the choice between *clear* or *clever*, go with the name that makes your podcast transparent. Clarity first, zany second.

When you research similar shows in *iTunes* and *ListenNotes* you'll see how the most popular shows within your niche or industry have names that make it obvious why you should listen. Does the name of your podcast speak to your perfect listener, rather than being quirky and a little bit unusual?

Another aspect to consider with your podcast's name is whether to include *your* name within the podcast title itself. When I rebranded I called my podcast *Inspiring Success Podcast with Anna Parker-Naples,* resulting in my name coming up in lots more searches. Later, I felt that *Entrepreneurs Get Visible* was about much more than me and should be found organically by those who aren't familiar with me and my personal story, so I leave my name out of the title but place it boldly in the visual branding for the show. Whichever method you choose, your name will be listed as the Show Host and still be searchable within podcast directories. I advise using your name as the name of the show only if you already have a significant following.

A few years ago, *iTunes* introduced a new ruling regarding names. A wave of new hosts with an understanding of dubious keyword search practices were putting other celebrity or influential podcasters' personal names in the name of their podcast ... essentially *keyword stuffing* someone else's name into the title in order to position their show inside searches for that big name. It is no longer allowable but I have recently seen podcasts using this method in the show description by stating that 'listeners who might like this [insert celebrity or expert name] show will like my show'.

Once you have a shortlist of names to weigh up, do some research. Check if there are any podcasts with similar or identical names to your idea. You must do this - it is important from a legal perspective and for recognizing how challenging it could be for your audience to find your podcast if its name is similar to another.

Your next step is to ensure the corresponding web

domain is available for purchase and that the social media handles aren't already in use. This is important because, as your podcast grows, your show's impact could really scale. Make sure you're not using someone else's trademark and branding. This may mean going back to the drawing board for a rethink, but it's worth it.

As you think about a name for your show, think also about the SEO terms you gathered during your research in Chapter 4. What does your perfect listener need to know? Why would they come to your show? Why would they be drawn to it? The name must make this blindingly obvious.

Once you have that shortlist, let your potential listeners, followers and connections in your current audience be part of the process in finalizing your decision. Run polls within your own *Facebook* group or someone else's online community. Tell them you're creating a podcast for a particular demographic and designated result. Ask them for feedback: 'Would you prefer option A or B?' Crowdsourcing responses matters as you design and develop your show. It helps those connected with you to join you on the journey of your podcast creation. It creates desire to know what's going on with your show, and anticipation for release. You can garner a keen audience weeks before you launch by sharing and including them in the process.

Podcast Description

Your research and SEO insight work will feed into your podcast description. Descriptions are important for piquing interest from the right listener. They influence how your show is filtered into categories and picked up in searches, how your podcast appears in *ListenNotes* and which categories you show up in inside *iTunes*. The description is often the first thing a potential listener will browse through to see if your show appeals to them. Make sure your show will come up in appropriate searches by having the correct keywords in your podcast description.

Artwork and Design

First impressions count. Your podcast artwork will be the first encounter people have with your show. A professional-looking appearance is fundamental. Looking as though you've knocked something together will do you no favours in winning listeners.

Head over to *iTunes* again to look at the current top-ranking shows in your podcast's category. Judge the effectiveness of the imagery. Notice colours, artwork and fonts shared by the most popular shows. Is there a style preference for the genre? Do the highest-ranking shows disrupt that pattern? Which images stand out on the web page? Be aware of the shows your podcast is likely to be positioned alongside should you launch successfully enough to be included in the *New Shows* or *Top Shows* sections within your chosen categories.

What do you notice when you look at the shows in your chosen category? What pulls you in? Which fonts can you read without effort? Which are almost illegible? What can't you make out or understand in the imagery? What do you have to examine closer to know about? Which images or styles capture your attention? Which photographs don't you like? Decide what appeals to you and what does not. Work out why.

There are some common trends amongst sizing and type of font. You'll see that information on artwork is legible even when it's reduced in size. On a mobile phone app- the most popular way to consume podcasts - some of these images are incredibly small. For your own artwork, ensure that your design and fonts translate equally as a large image or a tiny image inside an app on your phone.

For wording on the artwork, some podcasts simply display the show title. Others have more text, including a sub-title and/or the host's name on the podcast cover. Think again about the purpose of your podcast. How important is it that your name is displayed there? You may decide to keep your artwork clean and simple, highlighting the show's name only.

Notice when you are drawn to strong imagery. Personally, I prefer those with simplicity. Too much going on visually can feel messy and overwhelming. You'll see certain style preferences in artwork designs. Do you want to follow the majority or do something different? Your podcast should look as though it belongs to the genre, and should draw attention. Think about the main colours – your artwork should 'pop'.

I recently saw a poll on artwork in a *Facebook* group … in the initial designs the background colour was a pale pastel blue. It wasn't attention-grabbing. With crowdsourced feedback the intensity of the blue sky was adjusted, enabling the design to stand out along-side its counterpart shows.

Whether or not to include a picture of yourself is a style choice. It depends how far you are using your show as a personal brand-building vehicle. Is your following big enough to warrant that at time of launch? I do use a photograph of me on my podcast because a great deal of my messaging is about visibility and being seen. My face has to represent that. Additionally, I am using my podcast to catapult my personal brand. However, it is by no means a requirement … some experts argue that doing so wastes valuable 'real estate' on the artwork. They prefer to use big, bold text to make the purpose of the show obvious through its name. You may want more of a community atmosphere and feel that a photograph of you is not representative of, or appealing to, that community or group.

Will you include your own name on the podcast artwork? Again, what is the purpose of your podcast? Keep going back to that ... I've seen many shows start out with no host name - just the logo and the name of the show. With increased audiences the hosts rebranded to include their names. Whatever you initially decide on, nothing is set in stone. You have flexibility to change later.

Podcast Artwork Dimensions

When submitting your show to the main podcast directories, there are strict criteria to meet. Make sure that extremely small artwork can be seen and read on any device. Artwork file dimensions for *iTunes* are between 1400 by 1400 pixels, or the largest is 3000 by 3000 pixels. Your image must be square and saved as a JPEG or PNG file. The saved file size must be smaller than 500kb and you may need to use a file compression tool to ensure you can meet *iTunes* requirements.

Artwork Design Tools

If affordable, I recommend outsourcing the design of your podcast artwork to a professional designer. A designer will have a better understanding of what makes artwork stand out. Our podcast production agency can take care of this aspect for you too, including artwork for each individual episode, together with quotes from your show and artwork templates for promotional videos known as Audiograms. If budget does not allow, I'd recommend *Canva.com* and *Picmonkey.com* - online, easy to use design websites, both with ready-to-go template designs for podcasts and access to thousands of stock images.

A final word of warning about your podcast artwork - I strongly recommend that you don't use an image of a podcast microphone in your podcast artwork unless podcasting itself is your topic. So many people do this because they think podcast = microphone. Remember - your artwork should make it clear what your topic is. For example, if your podcast is about money, it would be more beneficial and appropriate to include something about money in the imagery rather than a picture of something that means nothing to your audience. In addition, do not incorporate *Apple*, *Google* or *Spotify* logos in your artwork. Your show will not be validated with *Apple* and will be prevented from going live.

Once you have a couple of mock-ups of your design ideas, crowdsource feedback from your audience and connections. Go into *Facebook* groups and ask what people think. Does this font work? Which colour pops? Which imagery works for you? It's important to gather responses from your target audience but it's also a way to stimulate interest and a feeling of inclusion in your podcast creation. Share the journey of your podcast creation from the outset so that you are seeding interest in your podcast and its launch, which we'll look at in much more detail in Chapter 12.

Intros and Outros

Your podcast's intro and outro are essentially the sound signature that listeners will quickly associate with its brand. The intro provides the next impression people have of your show beyond the artwork. In the opening seconds, a new listener will decide whether to continue listening …whether the style, vibe, sound appeals to them. You get one chance to make this impression. From the first moment of listening you should ensure the sound represents what your show is about. Embedding brand associations in your listener's mind is much easier during that introduction than anywhere else. I recently learned that 45% of people who will turn off your show, do so in the first five seconds due to poor quality audio, often before you have even spoken. The intro speaks volumes.

There are various options for the style of your intro. Whilst there are some more popular choices, there is no right or wrong.

Option 1: You could dive straight into the content with just your voice and words - no formal introduction. In the early days I chose this method, more out of a lack of appreciation for the potential of my podcast than a style choice. It is the simplest way to set up your show but lacks finesse.

Option 2: You could have a music-only introduction. Once the music fades, in comes your voice. This was my preference for my first podcasts. I had a short music track that was created specifically for my brand. It featured heavily in the accompanying meditations and trainings I delivered, so there was consistency in my audio across the board for my brand. Lasting approximately 10 seconds, I'd go straight into delivering the show after it played. Lacking a formal pre-recorded intro I scripted the beginning of each separate episode of my show: 'Welcome to *Inspiring Mummy Club Podcast*' or 'Welcome to *Inspiring Success Podcast*'.

Option 3: You could begin your show with a voice-over introduction. Usually this is mixed with a music bed underneath the vocal track. Further choices here include recording the intro with your own voice or employing a professional voiceover artist to create an introduction for your show. There are pros and cons to each style. A professional voiceover can make your show sleeker and is more common amongst American podcasts where the host is officially announced onto their own show. This can be effective for personal brand credibility building. Often, a male voice is used if the host is female, and vice versa. In my current show I use my own voice because not only am I capable and confident behind the microphone but I want my voice to be a major part of my brand.

I recommend going to your favourite podcast platform and finding at least five podcasts in your field that are close to the kind of show you want to create. Listen to the start of each one. Write down what you notice. How quickly did the music come in? How long did it take for the voice to start speaking? What style and length was the entire introduction? How long was it until the body of the show began, until you heard the content that you expected to hear? Did the initial audio represent the body of the show well or was there a disparity in pace and tempo? Listen to these back-to-back to hear what works for you. Notice the language they use in their intros, how they introduce themselves, the general ambience they create. Think about what you could do better. Think about the pace and the delivery, and if it is a good fit for the podcast genre.

I intended *Entrepreneurs Get Visible* to be like a shot of caffeine, a jolt of inspiration - and so I injected it with an upbeat energy. That intention is conveyed in the pace and delivery of my intro. Right from the start, people know what they're getting. What is your own intended delivery and style? If you have a relaxed natural laid-back style of speech, that's great, and many people will warm to you. But be cautious. A warm, welcoming, relaxed feel to your intro is all well and good, but it should not be too long. New listeners will switch off.

The ideal podcast intro should be no longer than 60 seconds. Whittle that down to under 30 for even more impact. Listeners want to get to the main content as soon as they can. A listener who finds a show they love will potentially binge listen to a back catalogue of previous episodes. If they are listening again and again to an intro that's a minute and a half long, perhaps longer, it can be enough to drive them to skip through your show.

Scripting Your Intro

As you listen to those five shows and their introductions, see if you can glean the listener's expectations. Is the script engaging? Do the words in the intro make it obvious what to expect? Is it dull? What first impressions have they created? Did they do a good job? Or were they ... BORING?!

Here is a sample of my current introduction for the *Entrepreneurs Get Visible* podcast:

'This is *Entrepreneurs Get Visible*, the podcast for people who want more impact, influence and income. I'm Anna Parker-Naples, and I'll be sharing with you proven methods from leading entrepreneurs that help you get visible as an authority in your field. Because anything's possible when you get visible.'

In just 49 words I convey who the podcast is for and what they will learn. The intro, including the music, is just 22 seconds long. It ends with a tagline that encapsulates my teachings: *Anything's possible when you get visible*. A tagline is useful for establishing the focus of your podcast. An effective tagline sticks in the listener's mind and is easily repeatable. The most compelling taglines include some form of rhythm or rhyme or alliteration.

Finally, script your own introduction. Include these key points: the title, what to expect from the show and brief information about yourself. 50 to 75 words is ample to keep within the time frames. Make every word you use calculated for effect.

Music

An intro with music gives your podcast a professional stamp. Visit online stock libraries and do a search into the kind of styles that might be appropriate. Sites such as *Audiojungle* and *Pond 5* allow you to purchase a license permitting you to incorporate the track of your choice for a certain period of time. Restrictions on downloads and channels apply, so make sure you purchase the applicable license.

You can search the thousands of tracks on these sites using keywords relating to your preferred style. Decide what kind of pace and tempo you want. Do not use music from a commercial track that you happen to like. It will get you into trouble and is not worth the hefty fine. If you cannot find a track that is exactly what you are looking for you can have bespoke audio created using freelancer sites such as *Fiverr* or *Upwork*.

Outro

Your outro (the tail end of your podcast) serves two purposes. First, it is the final piece of brand association that you'll leave your listeners with and it rounds off your episode completely. Second, it gives you an opportunity to give a final call to action to your listeners. How are you driving the activity of your listener?

Where are you taking them to? Do you want to lead them to a community? Do you want to lead to them to a lead magnet in exchange for an email address? Perhaps you want to ask them in your outro to subscribe, rate and review your show or recommend it to their friends.

For the outro style, again, you have these choices - music only or voice only? Or will you finish your episode at the conclusion of your interview? Think about the lasting impression you wish to create. In my current outro the music fades in underneath the end of the conversation. Then the scripted, pre-recorded outro begins, in which I invite and encourage listeners to a specific call to action. This might be a freebie, a checklist or a guide. I have a page on my website where all of the resources for my show, together with links to previous episodes and show notes are housed alongside my recommended resources and partners. Finally, the episode trails off with the last beats of my music - the last beat they hear is the sound signature that accompanies the branding of my podcast. How do you want people to feel as you close your show? The smallest details can leave an impression.

Podcast Spotlight

Grace Nelson & Charlotte Barrett, *Think. Create. Initiate.*

We started our podcast because we are passionate about empowering our audience with stories and strategies that can help them shift the needle on their entrepreneurial journey whilst building their business in small pockets of time - enabling them to know just what is possible.

Since launching we have reached a new audience that is growing globally weekly. We have interviewed amazing guests and grown our network. We have grown our *Facebook* group organically. We entered the highly competitive US charts and reached #14 in the *UK Entrepreneurship* charts. We have also developed relationships with influencers in our space who we have interviewed as guests.

Anna's support has been integral to our podcast journey which we are loving. We would not have launched successfully and ranked in the podcast charts without her guidance, support and encouragement to keep pushing through. Her knowledge and guidance have been key to us growing our visibility globally and getting our message out there, which was so important to us.

If you have a message, commit to sharing it with the world. Gain expert help and do not try and do it yourself. The results will be success and momentum. You will save yourself tons of time, money and disappointment by following a proven winning formula.

6

RECORDING EQUIPMENT

Sound quality is everything. Without it, listeners will switch off. It's as simple as that. But it doesn't have to be broadcast or Dolby surround sound Hollywood movie quality. After all, people are predominantly listening through a mobile phone which doesn't have the best speakers in the world. An amateurish-sounding podcast puts listeners off, though, and they won't return, no matter how informative, engaging or useful your content. In this chapter I will lead you through the basics of recording great quality audio to give your show the best chance of retaining hard-won listeners with all of your branding and design work.

Recording Environment

Make sure that your background environment is as noise-free and 'clean' as it can be. This will save you time in the editing process. The chief thing about good quality recording is the environment that you're recording in, not the microphone or fancy equipment. First, make sure that the space you plan to record in is in the quietest part of your home, that it is not cavernous and noisy and that there are minimal opportunities for sound waves to bounce around the room. Ideally, use a smaller room or enclosed space. Each room you record in has a different sound ambience. We don't usually notice with our naked ear, but when sound is picked up by a powerful microphone all sorts of anomalies can be amplified. For example, you would understand that a recording from inside your bathroom would sound tinny and echoey. This is due to the large amount of hard surfaces that the sound waves can bounce off (I promise I won't get more technical about how sound works than that!) The more muffled and padded a space is, the better chance you have of creating a good tone for your audio recordings. This is why acoustic sound panels are used in professional and many makeshift studios to absorb sound. When you're recording in your home or office, be aware of the environment around you. Soft furnishings or padding that you can bring into the room can help absorb some of that hard sound.

In practice, what this might look like is a room with lots of blankets, pillows, cushions and a carpet or rug on the floor near where you're recording. Instead of recording in the middle of a large, wooden-floored room, record in the corner of a smaller room that you can partially enclose. Surround the recording area, especially behind the microphone, with something to muffle the sound. This could be acoustic panels, an acoustic sound shield (available on *Amazon*) or even blankets or duvets. If not recording a video podcast explore areas of your home that might look less attractive but offer a richer sound experience - such as inside your wardrobe.

Test areas of your environment by recording the 'silence' in that space. Press record and physically leave the area for a minute or two so that your breathing and the movement of your clothing isn't picked up on the track. Once you have completed one test recording, move your set-up to a different location and repeat. Listen back with quality closed back headphones. Compare the room tone for clarity. There will be a discernible variation.

When you listen back to the test samples from various parts of your house, turn the volume up as high as is comfortable. You can hear absolutely every thing in the background - the rubbish truck in the next street, the noisy neighbours up the road inside their home, an airplane or train in the distance, traffic. Once you're aware of what's going on in your environment, position your microphone as far away from a window, door or any walls adjacent to troublesome spots as possible. Often, the centre of your house is a better place to record than near an external wall, or a wall that adjoins an area where you cannot control the environment's noise. Inside a cupboard may work well, or, if possible, surround yourself with acoustic panels like I do. Don't forget soft furnishings as an option!

Emergency recording situations

The following is an example of how you can create good quality audio with minimal equipment. I was once on holiday in France in the middle of nowhere. I received a call telling me I'd made it to the final selection process for a leading brand's interactive phone voice - you know the one ... I just can't say it due to a non-disclosure agreement. They needed audio urgently for their ultimate decision. I had no laptop with me but I did have my iPhone and a basic travel microphone that I could attach to my iPad. I knew that the background sound was vital, so I made a pillow fort inside the gite's wardrobe using all the blankets, duvets and pillows in the holiday home. By the time I was finished the producers and agencies involved had no clue that I wasn't in my usual set-up. You do not need a flash studio.

When attending conferences for voiceover talent across the world, the leading voices for commercials often head back to their hotel rooms to complete audio recordings. They put their duvets over their heads to create the best possible sound in the most challenging environment. I can assure you that when needs must and contracts depend on it, even the highest-paid audio professionals in the world use makeshift studios. It's just that no-one talks about it.

Another option if you are struggling for a quiet space is your car. Modern cars are designed with a degree of soundproofing. It's not ideal but if your neighbours are noisy it could work as a makeshift option. I've recorded tight turnaround commercials this way. It does mean there is more work to do in the edit, however.

Background noise

There are various *background* issues you should be aware of before you begin recording. First - computer noise. Turn off notifications and put your phone on airplane mode. In fact, your phone should be nowhere near where you are recording as sometimes it can create interference which you may not be aware of until afterwards. Also, the fan noise of your computer may kick in. Some computers are better for this than others. Turn off any applications and close any app windows that you aren't using whilst you record. Get into the habit of recording with headphones on in order to protect the integrity of your audio. Background noise can be removed in the edit to some degree but taking a few precautions in the first place will save you time, effort and energy. If you find that the fan is an issue for you, consider switching to a handheld voice recorder instead. This will allow you to record directly onto an SD card and transfer the files later. A popular choice is the *H4N Zoom* handheld recorder.

Be aware of background noise from radios and televisions playing in the distance. Be aware of people talking in the background, dishwashers, washing machines. I recommend, particularly if you're doing an audio-only podcast, a portable sound booth - otherwise known as a *microphone isolation shield* - behind your microphone. These in no way provide soundproofing but can improve the quality of the audio in challenging set-ups. If you want to get serious, create a professional studio in your home (honestly, though, you do not need this to get started).

Microphones

The microphone market is huge and you could spend hours choosing yours, as well as much of your hard-earned cash. The reality is that for under $100 you could get going with a robust microphone that sounds great. The most important thing is to get started with something you can afford and think about upgrading later.

There are two types of microphone, and the following explains how they interact with your computer or other audio interface.

XLR vs USB

It used to be the case that XLR microphones were accepted as the only professional quality microphones on the market. They were considerably more powerful than USB microphones and are still commonly referred to as 'studio-quality' microphones. They require an additional piece of hardware to connect to a computer - an audio interface. A USB microphone simply plugs straight into your Mac or PC and you're ready to go.

When these entered the market, audio professionals saw them as inferior in tone and sound capabilities because they didn't require additional kit to create quality, clear audio. Whilst initially this may have been the case, over the past decade, advancements in technology have resulted in improvements in the recording capacity of USB microphones. I'm going a little against the grain here by telling you this, but to all but the trained ear, a good USB microphone is indistinguishable from a lower end XLR microphone.

If you're just starting out, I would go with a good USB microphone – it will probably be sufficient for your entire podcasting career. However, if you love your technology, start with a XLR. You will also get better results if you choose a microphone designed for voice recordings rather than music, some of which are designed to pick up background noise.

Dynamic vs. Condenser Microphones

The two types of microphone commonly used for podcasting are *dynamic* or *condenser*. These sound moderately different, so personal preference plays a big part in your choice. However, there are some technical differences that are worth knowing, even for the least tech-minded podcaster.

For both dynamic and condenser microphones, how they connect to your recording device will inform your choice, as this could be USB or XLR. Second, condenser microphones have better response to high frequencies than dynamic ones. This results in a crisp, detailed sound. However, it can be a problem for recording at home as a condenser mic may pick up too much of the *shhh* sound from air vents or extra noises from the lips and tongue.

Advantages of a dynamic microphone

Dynamic microphones are relatively simple in design and to manufacture and so tend to be cheaper. They can provide excellent sound quality and good specifications in all areas of microphone performance. You can position yourself nice and close to a dynamic microphone and take advantage of something called the *proximity effect* which gives you that intimate, classic radio sound with a nice low-end bass frequency (essentially a boost to the bass levels).

Dynamic microphones can also handle extremely high sound levels. They are generally less sensitive by design and there are some benefits to this. For example, they are more forgiving if there are sudden bursts of increased volume. Dynamic microphones are generally unaffected by extremes of temperature or humidity and can have a durable lifespan. On the whole they tend to be more rugged in design, with a sturdy and resilient construction, able to withstand rough handling and on-the-go recording (although why you would ever want to be rough with your precious recording equipment baffles me!) They are often designed with the intention of only picking up the sound directly in front of them. Dynamic microphones do not require what is known as *phantom power* (an additional power supply) in order to work.

Dynamic microphones, with their low starting price, are a good choice for podcasting. Since you are recording only your voice, they will produce a great sounding podcast, especially true if you can get nice and close for those low-end frequencies. They are also preferable if you have a noisy room, loud co-hosts or a multiple mic set-up. Each person can have their own dedicated dynamic mic to record a clean conversation with less of the extraneous noise being picked up.

Disadvantages of a dynamic microphone

They are less sensitive by design. The heavy microphone diaphragm and wire coil limits the movement of the assembly. This in turn restricts the frequency and response of the microphone. Dynamic microphones are not as suitable for recording musical instruments, especially with higher frequencies and harmonics such as a violin.

Advantages of a condenser microphone

Without going into too much detail, the condenser microphone has more intricate, delicate parts than the dynamic microphone. This means the internal mechanisms can move more easily and quickly in tune with sound waves, allowing more nuances to be picked up and resulting in superior sound quality

Condensers have a wider frequency response and can pick up sudden bursts of sound energy even if placed sufficiently away from them. They can, however, distort the audio if the sound source (in the case of your podcast, your mouth) is too close and too loud. Generally, condenser microphones offer much higher sensitivity and record more depth and warmth in the voice.

They have a more accurate interpretation of the sound and when used a little further away from your mouth deliver a natural conversational tone, rather than a tone that can seem a bit sterile and distant. This richness can be very pleasant to listen to and can make your voice sound frankly AMAZING.

Disadvantages of condenser microphones

Using a condenser microphone increases the likelihood of picking up sound from co-hosts and the room in general. When using a condenser microphone, be mindful of how many people are talking at any one time and make sure the room is extremely quiet. On the whole, a condenser microphone is better suited for a recording environment that has been treated with professional grade acoustic studio foam rather than a moderately adapted space in your home or office. To put it another way, I would use my condenser microphone in my studio (where it would sound brilliant) but not in my open plan kitchen (where it would pick up so much from the room around me and make my voice sound tinny).

Condenser microphones are not as sturdy as dynamic microphones and need to be handled carefully. They may not make a good portable choice for recording on the go. Due to the complexity of their internal mechanisms, they can be considerably more expensive. They usually require *phantom power and* are more complex than dynamic microphones, being more adversely affected by extremes of temperature and humidity.

To summarise, a dynamic mic is a great microphone to start with and a good overall microphone for podcasting. It can provide the same or better audio quality at a lower price. You may not need a perfectly acoustically-treated room or studio to use a dynamic microphone.

On the other hand, if you can spend more and have a good recording room/studio, then a condenser microphone will certainly give you a richer sound quality. Every make and model of microphone will capture your voice sound a little bit differently from the next and some microphones are more suited to male voices - and vice versa - due to how they react to high and low frequencies. Choose the mic that fits your personal requirements and level of expertise with audio, your budget and makes your voice sound pleasant to listen to and you won't go wrong. Getting started is better than perfect.

Polar Patterns

Your microphone may have settings known as *polar patterns*. When recording alone you should choose what is known as a *cardioid setting*. This setting picks up sounds directly in front of the microphone and delivers a rich, full-bodied tone. Your microphone may also have a *bi-directional* capability, ideal for an interview with one other person sitting across from you, and, finally, there may be an *omnidirectional* function allowing for quality recording of a 'round the table' style discussion.

Stands, Boom Arms and Shock Mounts

Again, dependent upon the microphone you invest in, you may have to purchase an additional stand. Your choices here are a *table-top stand* or a *boom arm*. The simplest to set up is a table stand. One of the downsides to having a table-top stand is the impulse to lean in and down to speak into the microphone. I recommend putting a book or a block underneath it to lift the microphone so that you don't have to drive your voice downwards. It can be tempting to collapse your posture which in turn affects the quality of your voice and breath capacity.

A boom arm stand can be positioned so that your microphone is in front of your face at a small distance - far enough away that you don't have to think about it or strain your neck by reaching up to speak into it. These are usually clamped to a table or desk. Quality microphones can be robust and heavy. If you have invested a significant amount, don't scrimp on the stand. It may not be sufficient in strength to support the microphone long-term.

Shock Mounts

If you do go for an XLR microphone, especially a powerful, sensitive condenser, then you may need a piece of equipment called a *shock mount*. The mount absorbs the impact of movement around the microphone, preventing it from picking up all sorts of wobbles and distortions that can affect the audio quality. Shock mounts are often specific to the microphone so before you purchase your mic, check if one is required as standard.

You can see my up-to-date recommendations for microphones, stands, shockmounts and headphones here: *www.annaparkernaples.co.uk/podcastchecklist*.

Pop Shields

A *pop shield* (also known as a *pop filter* or *pop screen*) is a noise protection filter for microphones. It serves to reduce or eliminate 'popping' sounds caused by the mechanical impact of fast-moving air on the microphone during recorded speech. A typical pop filter is composed of layers of material stretched over a circular frame and often includes a clamp and flexible mounting bracket. Metal pop filters use a fine mesh metal screen in place of the nylon and newer studio condenser microphones have an integral pop filter built into their design.

A pop shield is clamped in front of your microphone. It stops *plosives* - your 'p' and 'b' sounds when you speak - from ejecting air into the microphone,

which can distort your audio and is not easily rectifi-
able. The pop shield also prevents saliva or spittle from
reaching your microphone and can lengthen the life of
your equipment. An alternative to a pop shield is a
wind cover which sits over the top of the microphone. If
you were recording outside a wind cover would protect
the microphone from all angles. For a standard indoor
recording set-up, a pop shield is sufficient.

Audio Interfaces and Mixers

I know, I know, this is getting way more technical than
you probably want, so I'll be brief. If you choose a
USB microphone, you have everything you need. If
you choose a XLR microphone, you will need some
extra kit.

Audio Interface

With a XLR microphone you will also need to use an
audio interface. This is a piece of hardware that connects
to your USB port and expands and improves the sonic
capabilities of your recordings giving you the ability to
connect professional microphones to your computer.
An audio interface can greatly improve the sound
quality and make your voice 'zing'. When you record
new audio and then listen through high quality

speakers or professional grade headphones, the inter-face will reproduce a more accurate representation of the sounds you make. With a good microphone and a great audio interface your voice will sound incredible. Believe me, a great audio set-up will leave you eager to hear more of your dulcet tones!

Mixer

A mixer gives you more control over the audio in your recording. You can mix, mute, solo, adjust volumes and much more. It's generally all done live - while you're recording – and is quite seamless. For podcasters who want to record a live radio-style show, a mixer is must.

To pull off a live-style show, you should be comfort-able with your equipment and know the flow of your show and have any music or sound effects ready to bring in at the right moment. This will reduce the time-consuming post-production process greatly if you wish to develop your production skills.

For the vast majority of you just getting started, a mixer is not necessary. An audio interface is an option for your show to have excellent audio quality in combi-nation with a XLR mic, and a USB mic will be abso-lutely fine for a painfree start in podcasting.

I promise - that's as technical as I'm going to be anywhere in this book. And breathe.

Headphones

When recording a podcast it's important to use headphones to listen for static, loudness and other issues. You should opt for *closed-back* headphones so that the microphone doesn't pick up audio bleeding (sound coming from the headphones). Some podcasters don't like to record with headphones on but it is a practice that I urge you to integrate into your recording routine. If your pipes start gurgling or there is a plane overhead, your ear won't pick it up but your headphones will.

Another reason for wearing headphones is to monitor all those natural mouth noises that happen when your voice gets sticky and dry through too much talking. You will hear when you need to drink some water in order to give yourself the best chance of a clean recording, free from noisy saliva sounds.

If you choose to forgo headphones (which may appeal if you are recording video content), use quality headphones for editing purposes as they will allow you to hear all sorts of pops, clicks and extraneous sounds.

Recording on the Go

I am passionate about making podcasting a streamlined part of your everyday life. You have a couple of options for recording when you are out and about - either on your own or when the opportunity for an impromptu in-person interview arises at a conference or other networking event. What I'm about to suggest is a good option for getting started with creating podcast content on a budget.

A quality clip-on microphone, sometimes referred to as a *lavalier microphone,* can be a great addition to your handbag (or manbag ... or briefcase ... does anyone even use those anymore?!) It can be attached directly to your cell phone (in some instances an adapter may be required, depending on your handset). My favourite clip-on microphones allow you to attach an additional clip-on mic to the set-up, allowing both sets of audio to be monitored, recorded and edited directly on the same phone. For me, this makes going to conferences or recording when I'm traveling much more achievable.

I record *Facebook Lives* that I want to repurpose into podcast content on my phone via the clip-on microphone. Occasionally I record podcasts when I'm walking the dog, so I make sure I inform my listeners of what's going on around me. I take them on the journey with me, so to speak.

Handheld recorders

Many professional podcasters use a handheld recording device. They are more of an investment than a basic USB microphone set-up, so may not be the best initial spend when you're just beginning but are worth knowing about. Typically, you record onto an *SD card* which can hold up to eight hours of content. The handheld recorder has a long battery life, much better than that of your phone, which is equally portable, but prone to use battery life quickly and leave you at the mercy of pings, unexpected calls and notifications. Most examples have microphones built into them as well as options to attach multiple XLR or clip-on microphones. This is useful if you are delivering a speech on stage and want to capture the presentation. A handheld recorder such as the *H4N Pro Zoom* also acts as an audio interface which can improve the quality and tone of your recording. If you are serious about podcasting you might like to give a handheld recorder a go. You will require an adapter to import the data from the SD card onto your computer later.

Recording Software

For production of your podcast you'll need audio editing software for both recording and editing. I recommend you begin with *Audacity* - a free download for both the Mac and PC. *Audacity* has all the functions necessary for a quality podcast. There are many more sophisticated editing software options, most of which will be overly complex for your needs. The industry standard is *Adobe Audition* which requires a monthly subscription although it does come as part of the *Adobe Creative Suite*. Alternatively there is *Pro Tools*. I promise you – you will not need anything so complex.

If you have an iPhone then I would recommend *Twisted Wave Lite*, my audio software of choice for on-the-go recordings. It's easy to edit on your phone and simple to forward longer tracks with larger files using its online system. This means you can save the audio file without taking up precious storage space on your phone.

This chapter has been a long one but the message is - if you want to keep it simple, go with a USB mic and your computer. If you're broke, use your phone and a clip-on mic until you can afford to upgrade. If you know you mean business with your podcast, get a XLR mic and an audio interface. Boom. That's it, in a nutshell. The most important thing about recording equipment for your podcast? That you actually get started. Refine later.

A note about production values: the quality of your output matters if you want to be at the top of the tree in your field. If you are serious about creating a podcast that is powerful and flawless in its delivery and which will place you on a level with world class leaders, podcasting is the same as every other field of business. Do you want to be entry level, mid-level or heavy weight in your podcast excellence? There is a way to podcast for every rung of the ladder. Here, I've covered how to start. You can refine the process by seeking expert advice and consultancy. If you want to be amongst the podcasting elite, get in touch.

Podcast Spotlight

Laura Moss, *Moments to Inspire and Connect*

I started my podcast to be more visible, give others a voice and enjoy connecting with people whilst providing inspiration to others. *The Podcast Membership* was invaluable. The content helped me, from creating my ideal listener to launching, growing and monetizing my podcast. And the amazing community she has created in the membership *Facebook* group provided support. The members help with questions, support you in obstacles if they have already launched and help grow your podcast by getting behind the launch. I would not have launched without Anna and certainly wouldn't have reached #14 in the *Entrepreneurship* charts. In fact, I would have talked myself out of it and not had the confidence to believe I could do it. Simple things such as the equipment and what was the best thing to buy would have held me back from the beginning, let alone the daunting thought of editing. But three months on from Anna's challenge and I have purchased the equipment, recorded, edited and got my podcast onto all the right platforms.

Podcasting has given me another platform to be more visible. Social media is a great platform but when listening to an interview with someone it really helps get to know them. Not only are my listeners able to relate to those stories and learn something from their knowledge, they are also getting to know me which is building that like, know and trust.

Do it! There is no time like the present. It doesn't have to be daunting. It can be fun and life-changing with the right support behind you. People need to hear what you have to say

7

RECORDING TECHNIQUE

The first time I used a studio-grade professional microphone and headphones, I was hooked. I was recording a commercial and several promos for an animation series and the accompanying dolls soon to hit the toy stores. I was pleasantly surprised to hear how a great microphone can amplify the resonance and lower tones in my usually high-pitched voice and make my voice sound richer and fuller than I ever imagined. Conversely, it was strange to hear my recorded voice on playback through headphones. It didn't sound like me, or at least not how I usually experience my voice. Most people don't like the sound of their voice when it is recorded and it can take a while to become accustomed to. I promise you, though, that as much as you fret about your voice - its tone, pitch and accent - no-one listening to you will be considering those matters.

They will be focused on the content you deliver. In fact, as humans we are drawn to quirks, foibles and imperfections in others. It helps to build a sense of rapport - invaluable for building a community of raving fans of your show.

In this chapter I will introduce you to some recording techniques which will help you podcast to the best of your ability. We'll discuss ideal microphone placement, mouth noise and how to get rid of it, ongoing vocal care and how this can improve your podcast. Finally, I'll talk about voice confidence and how it affects your delivery and the 'performance' element of your podcast.

In the previous chapter I briefly covered how the kind of microphone stand you use, and its location, can affect how you deliver the sound into the microphone. You should ensure that your microphone is as close to parallel with your mouth as possible. If you have a boom arm or a swivel mount stand, adjust it so that the microphone is directly in front of your face - six to 12 inches away - without obstructing your line of vision. Try to avoid stretching your neck to reach the microphone as this can cause vocal damage and neck and shoulder tension.

If using a table stand I recommend raising it by putting it on a block or a book so that the microphone is level with your mouth. Again, position the microphone six to 12 inches from your mouth. Ensure that your speech is driven forwards into the microphone rather than driving downwards. Check that you're not speaking off to one side or the other, too close, too far away. After doing a few test recording runs, listen back through headphones to the sound quality you're getting. You'll know when you hit what is known as 'the sweet spot' — when you just sound richer and fuller. In playback, if necessary, adjust the *gain* (the level of input from the microphone sound) so that the *waveforms* (the squiggly lines that move when you are speaking) on the recording software aren't peaking and distorting (I'll go into *peaking* later on). Play around with your distance to make sure the audio sounds great.

Become hyper-sensitive to surrounding noise. Make sure the traffic isn't loud, that it's not rush hour, there are no drivers beeping horns or ambulances flashing past. If there is a lot of traffic outside your window, record in a quieter space in the house or choose a less busy time of day. Make sure the toilet hasn't just been flushed in your house or a neighbour's. Make sure your appliances aren't noisy - microwave, dishwasher, washing machine, vacuum cleaner. With pets, do your best to quieten or placate them before you begin recording. A dog padding up and down outside your door or a hamster scrabbling on its wheel can ruin the best of takes - those pet noises can be picked up on a sensitive microphone even from adjacent rooms. My absolute favourite noise pollution is when the rubbish truck trundles slowly down my road, followed by builders working on a house up the street starting up a pneumatic drill. You'll be alert to external noise like never before. And don't get me started on people who decide to MOW THEIR LAWN just as I'm about to begin an interview!

There is also nothing more frustrating than your perfectly good recording being interrupted by notifications going off, your phone pinging, the timer on your watch. Make sure those electronic noises are turned off by yourself and your interviewee. Close down your email system, your *LinkedIn*, *Facebook*, *Google* tabs. Make sure, too, that other people in your household know when you are going to record (I've trained my children and husband into utter silence when they know I'm recording). Ask that they are mindful of the noise they are making in other rooms. In my household, my children watch TV or their tablets with earbuds even if three, four or five rooms away. Sound can bleed through into even the most robust recording studio set-up, so do your best to minimize issues.

Mouth noise

Creating a lot of audio content will show you how noisy you are when you speak. This might be *pops* or *clicks*, little vocal mannerisms or idiosyncrasies that you're not generally aware of. The times you stumble or stutter will seem amplified when you listen back. These are all perfectly normal and mouth noise can be combatted in many ways.

First, consider what you eat and drink. Being hydrated and aware of what you consume before you record will result in fewer clicks and pops. It also means less work to do in the edit stage - always a bonus. My top tip for dealing with mouth noise is to drink a lot of water, not only immediately before you do your recording, but increasing your water consumption the day before a batch of podcast interviews. Aiming for a minimum of two litres per day can improve the quality of your voice dramatically. It will keep your vocal folds hydrated and flexible and allow your mouth to work at its optimum level. Keep water with you in your recording area (but please ensure it is in a bottle with a lid to avoid spillages on your precious equipment). Sometimes, as you do a lot of talking, your mouth can become 'sticky' - pause recording, have a drink and return once your mouth is refreshed.

The consistency of our saliva changes according to

what we've consumed. In addition, caffeine can dry our mouths considerably. Our mouths combat this by producing saliva of a particular consistency in order to alleviate that dryness. Milk-based food and drink products, for instance, can create more of a mucal type saliva thickness. I would avoid both milk and caffeine until after your recording session.

If you do notice significant mouth noise, there are two things you can do: the first is take a bite of an apple - flesh only as the skin could get caught in your teeth. Apple flesh quickly helps produce more saliva, with a cleaner quality than water. The other quick way to alter your saliva levels is to chew gum. Those first few chews help to clean your mouth and make it feel fresh. Once the saliva glands have done their job remove the chewing gum and you're ready to record.

Warming Up Your Voice

You might be surprised to learn how much benefit there is in warming up your voice for simply recording a podcast episode. It's an important habit to form. The more speaking work you do, the more pressure you put on your vocal folds and throat. The more you warm up, however, the more clarity of speech you will have and it removes pressure from some of the vital areas of your voice production instrument. You can warm up by humming - performing singing drills by humming up and down the scale - and articulation exercises, e.g. tongue twisters. Exercises like this prepare your tongue, jaw and lips, together with all of the muscles in your face and neck, so that your diction is much sharper and less likely to damage your vocal folds. They also result in fewer sore throats through speaking for extended periods. You will be much clearer in delivery and your speech less sloppy and it will be easier for your listeners to understand what you're saying. Warm-ups are particularly useful if you plan to record in the morning. After sleep, our muscles are lazy. Do a few warm-up exercises to stretch out your mouth, jaw and tongue. Do some tongue twisters to improve the quality of your consonants. Get into the habit of warming up whenever you plan to do any recording work.

Clothing and Accessories

Clothing rustles are a total nuisance in your audio. Unwanted sounds can arise from earrings, necklace, watch or bracelet jingling away and these rustles can't always be removed in the edit. Generally, softer fabrics are better for recording. Years ago I went to a London studio for a recording for a television programme. I'd bought some new boots and gave them their first outing that day. Unbeknownst to me the synthetic material of the boots rubbed and squeaked the whole way through the recording and nobody spotted it until afterwards. You can imagine how popular I was. I never made that mistake again.

Movement

It's easy to form bad habits when you start out. Our natural mannerisms are often accelerated when we're nervous. Be aware of tapping your foot, wiggling your pen or moving your hands or body. Hand gesticulations are fine - it's natural to have some physical movement as you express yourself. But you must make sure you're not bashing anything in the room around you, knocking the desk, the computer, or, particularly, the microphone and its stand. Foot taps or wiggling in your chair are all captured by the microphone because it's a powerful instrument. Make sure your chair isn't squeaking, your shoes aren't creaking - give yourself the best chance of a clean recording.

Steaming

If doing a lot of voice work and potentially back-to-back recordings consider *steaming* your voice. You can buy vocal steamers – they cover your mouth and/or nose as you breathe into them and the steam clears your mouth and nasal passages. It softens and moisturizes your vocal folds keeping them flexible, healthy and strong. If you suffer from colds, steaming can help. Talking a lot without looking after your voice can cause long-term irreparable damage. In my early actor training at drama school I was forced to stop speaking for a three month period due to overstrain through inefficient warm-ups and poor vocal technique. Believe me, for someone who loves to communicate it was tough! If you give presentations, speak on stage or create podcasts consider establishing and maintaining an ongoing vocal care regime.

Vocal Care

Your voice is your instrument and if you were to lose it or damage it long-term, this would change your life. I am now fastidious about warming up and using alternative products to heal and protect my voice. I am attuned to the early warning signs of inflammation, vocal tiredness and throat pain. Manuka honey contains antiseptic and antibacterial qualities. It is an effective way to protect your voice and heal your throat. I tend to use it in a drink - one teaspoon in hot water. Additionally, if I have some, I'll add in one or two drops of Bee Propolis. You can purchase Bee Propolis and high-grade Manuka honey from most health food stores. It has saved my voice and repaired short-term irritation quicker than anything else I have tested and tried.

Vocal Confidence

Finally, a word or two about vocal confidence. Many people find speaking into a microphone inhibiting. They worry about how they come across, think that they have to speak differently, that they have to slow down, that they have to become robotic in order to be understood. They worry, when they hear themselves back, that they sound boring or too full on. Or, quite commonly, that they sound much younger and consequently won't be taken seriously. This is because when we hear our voices naturally, we're listening to it through all of the bones in our skull, creating a different level of resonance. When we hear our voice externally, it sounds like a distorted version of ourselves. If you find this off-putting, remember that your podcast is not really about *you*. It is about giving that value, building that community. It is about giving knowledge, experience and connection to your perfect listener. Conversely, as listeners, we're often drawn to imperfections. We like that it makes a host human and we feel drawn to their vulnerabilities. Have faith in that when you create your content. It does not have to be scripted. It is normal to stumble. It is acceptable to be you. Remember, too, that you can edit out a lot of the parts you don't like, should you decide to.

The more you get in front of the microphone and hear your voice after it has been fully edited and mastered, the quicker you'll become accustomed to how your recorded voice sounds. Keep going - even if you hate what you hear. Your voice is fine, your accent is fine. Everyone can understand you (especially if you have done your warms-ups and tongue twisters). You just need to trust your content and make a great podcast. Trust that your message needs to be heard and concentrate on getting it out into the big wide world.

Podcast Spotlight

Bron Webster, *The MS Show*

For the MS community we need something that is UK-voiced and independent of affiliation with pharma/lifestyle companies. For me, podcasting is a non-time-dependent platform meaning as a person with MS, I can work when the health sun is shining.

Anna's support has made podcasting a

reality for me. It's something I considered a couple of years ago but did not know how to progress. From understanding the technology and the equipment through to legal considerations and working out the aims of the podcast the information has been relevant, practical and accessible. I can't forget the self-belief Anna instils. I learned to start and perfect later. Without Anna's support this would never have happened for me and I know that podcasting would have remained on my list of things for the future. Without Anna, the MS Community wouldn't have another voice. Podcasting simply would not have happened.

Already, podcasting is beginning to give me a platform. It has given me a reason to seek out publicity. It has created interest and has increased my online visibility. This is within one month of launching. Quite simply - seek out Anna, join *The Podcast Membership* and absorb as much as you can.

8

RECORDING YOUR SHOW

Creating a podcast episode is not simply about switching on the microphone and talking. Consider the impact you want to have on the listener, what will draw them in and make them want to stay. For your business, think about the result you want to achieve from each and every episode. Is there a product to mention, a community you are growing or a specific lead magnet to drive people to download?

For each episode, start with the end in mind. Delivering your topic is much more purposeful when you understand that each episode title can be crafted to include keywords and search terms that your perfect listener is already looking for. Every title of *Entrepreneurs Get Visible* has been researched for SEO capability and so should yours if your podcast is to help build your listenership and your business.

Before recording a solo episode, draft a rough version of the episode flow - how you'll introduce the topic, resources you'll reference and their corresponding links, personal anecdotes relevant to the topic. Draft it in note-form - I urge you NOT to script anything (except your intro). You'll sound stilted and listeners will detect that you are reading. Do your prep work, make bullet-point notes, trust your expertise and experience, and go with the flow.

So far, you've planned your episode, plugged in your mic and put your headphones on (yes, even when it's just you). Now it's time to get recording.

Record Solo Episodes

There are many editing software programmes to choose from, some with a hefty price tag, some with complex and advanced functionality and some with simplicity and ease of use in their design. To prevent overwhelm, my suggestion for getting started is *Audacity*. It'*s* free, available on both Mac and PC and allows you to create everything you need for a quality audio.

If you're looking for software that's more sophisticated or want to go with an editing industry standard package, a couple of options are *Adobe Audition* and *Pro Tools*. Both require a monthly fee and I guarantee that as a podcaster you will use only a fraction of what they offer. If you're already subscribed to *Adobe Creative Suite*, you will probably have the *Adobe Audition* professional workstation included, so check what you already have access to.

For *Audacity*, simply download the software and install it onto your computer. Open the *Audacity* app, ready to begin a new track. First, select the correct microphone and check that it is highlighted at the top of the screen on the *Audacity* dashboard. My advice is to plug in your USB microphone (or audio interface or mixer if you are using a XLR) BEFORE your open up the software rather than once the app is open, as occasionally it doesn't register the microphone as available to select.

Audacity has a panel with basic and familiar navigation tools - *record*, *pause* and *stop* buttons. For voice recordings, record in mono (rather than stereo) and with the settings: 44,100 hertz (Hz), with a 16 bit float. These should be selected as standard when you open *Audacity* - if not they can be adjusted under the *Project Rate* tab at the bottom of the screen.

When recording, make sure that you always record some blank room sound before you begin speaking. This is important for the edit. I recommend having somewhere between 10 and 30 seconds of room tone before you begin your podcast content. The best way to do this is to get a sample of the room without you in it, literally out of the room with the door shut. That way your breathing and movement sounds will not be picked up. This will enable you to eliminate background noise from your audio later, leaving a much cleaner voice recording.

Have a play around with *Audacity*. Get used to the *record, delete* and *pause* functions. Do this a few times in advance of attempting the first official recordings for your show. The more confidence and familiarity you have with the technology, the more relaxed you will be, and this will come across in your delivery and performance.

When saving your audio, do not *save* the file into *Audacity*. Instead, export it. There are several options for file type. At this stage, having only recorded the audio and being not yet ready to edit the track, export it as a .wav file. A .wav file is often referred to as a *lossless file* as, unlike a .mp3 or .mp4 it has not been compressed to reduce its size, therefore more of the nuances are left intact. A .wav is much higher quality than a .mp3 and whether you are planning to do your edit yourself or send it to an editor, your raw audio should be as good quality as possible. Once you've completed a full edit, mixed and mastered the audio, you will then export it as a .mp3 for uploading into your podcast host and getting it into *iTunes and other podcast directories*.

For storing saved and exported files, I am a fan of *Dropbox*. Audio files can take up considerable room on your hard drive and I would recommend saving them somewhere more secure. *Dropbox* makes storing files in the cloud seamless and is particularly beneficial if other people are involved in your podcast workflow, such as outsourcers or a podcast production agency performing the functions of editing, show notes creation and social media posts connected with your show. This is how I work with clients in our podcast production agency. Once files are uploaded our team can take over the more in-depth processes. Your job remains focused on delivering useful and engaging content. The experts can do the spit and polish.

When practising your recordings take note of the squiggly lines that represent your voice as you speak. These are called *waveforms*. Ideally, these should appear fairly balanced in the middle of the visual representation of the track. Make sure they're not tiny and not really close to the centre line, and equally that they're not peaking at the top of the track guidelines. If I were too close to my microphone or shouted into it, the waveforms would go beyond the top and/or bottom of the guidelines. The audio would not be usable as it can't be easily repaired in the edit stage. Find the middle ground where you are not recording too loudly or too quietly. Waveforms that are too close to the line require a lot of sound amplification later on to make the audio useable. Depending on your microphone type and set-up, you can adjust the gain levels from your microphone to achieve the ideal sound, or from within the *Audacity* dashboard itself.

Editing processes are challenging to explain in words alone. If you would like more support we have trainings inside *The Podcast Membership*. However, we'll cover much more about *Audacity* (applies to other recording software applications too) later in the *Editing* Chapter. For now, trust yourself to explore and hone your recording skills. Keep your headphones on and you'll judge for yourself when your voice sounds as though you have hit the 'sweet spot.'

Interview Podcasts

The guest interview format has many benefits, not least the sharing of knowledge, value and story. This allows you to piggyback off other experts in terms of their connections, audience and specialized topics to make fantastic, powerful connections that often lead to collaboration, recommendations and referrals. By nurturing those relationships you increase the chances of your guests sharing your podcast episode with their audience via social media and their mailing list.

How to choose your guests

Go back to your *perfect listener avatar* - *w*hat do they want to learn? Who do they want to feel connected to? What stories do they want to be inspired by and what knowledge do they feel they don't have? Then revisit the purpose of your podcast.

If it is to increase your profile, reach, authority, focus on booking guests who are one or two steps ahead of you in your industry or even amongst the most established leaders within your field. Choosing guests becomes a strategic decision. Who listeners hear and see you with is powerful, and effective positioning. Make it intentional.

Where should you look for interesting, engaging guests? Newsflash - people who listen to your podcast listen to other podcasts, too. (I know, what a surprise!). If they've loved listening to someone on your podcast they'll likely follow them elsewhere. Many leading podcasters, entrepreneurs and business owners understand that podcast guesting is a great way to build listeners. There's definitely an art form and strategy behind how to profit from podcast guest appearances, though - something we cover in considerable detail in *The Podcast Membership*

Your perfect guest

What would make a *perfect guest avatar*? What value will they bring to your audience? What topics would be compelling? What kind of insights, tips and tricks might you like them to share? What knowledge? Once you have an idea of that it's worth doing some solid research in order to build a list of potential intervie-wees. Within a few months your initial ideas on guests will be exhausted. In this creation phase, when your interest, engagement and enthusiasm are high, having those ideas lined up and ready to go will be a blessing.

A mistake I made in the early days was to title the episode with only the name of the guest, giving no indication of the subject matter. Lead with the topic and include the guest's name as an addition. This way you are giving potential listeners an answer to a problem rather than inviting them to a general chitchat with someone they may have never heard of. I recently polled my audience and overwhelming they agreed that a compelling interesting topic was what led them to one episode over another.

I would recommend you begin your research for guests in *Google*. Note which people and websites are listed when you search the keywords you discovered in your earlier research. An alternative is to go on to *Apple* podcasts and search under the same category as your podcast. See if there are guest names that appear repeatedly for the topics you would like to include. Podcast hosts that you might like to interview are usually open to guesting, so include them in your guest lists.

Another valuable resource for planning guests is *Amazon*. Find authors who are writing about the topics you'll be focusing on. Business-minded authors will be keen to get in front of your audience – they understand that it's important to continually promote their book. You may be surprised at how many authors, even some household names, will say yes to an interview when a new book release is imminent. Check if their book is available for pre-order on *Amazon*, or find out by following them on social media. If your podcast has the right target audience for them they will be able to promote that new book. Podcast guesting is a vital part of a book launch strategy within a month either side of release and savvy authors use it to springboard their readership.

Another recommendation is to look up conferences in your niche. Visit conference websites and see who the speakers have been over the past couple of years. By being part of the conference line-up, you'll know that they are accomplished speakers carving a mark for themselves in your industry. Check their bios for ideas on their specialist subjects and what they're passionate about. This is valuable information for when you reach out to them.

Approaching Potential Guests

First, swot up on them. Do some online stalking on *LinkedIn*, *Google* and inside *iTunes*. If they are a podcast host, clicking on their show details in *iTunes* will give you a web address for the podcast. On the contact page you will find their email address. If you already have someone's *LinkedIn* connection you might get better results from a private message conversation with them about their work and any episodes, videos or books of theirs you have enjoyed. Once you have struck up that conversation, the most effective and professional way to propose an interview remains via email. It gives your request more gravitas and indicates that you take your podcast production values seriously.

It's also worth going into the *Facebook* groups where you have been garnering connections and asking who they would recommend as guests. Request introductions where applicable. I've sourced some brilliant people this way. Once you have a few potential guests, make sure they are right for your show by gathering more information. Create an online form - there are various services you can use such as *Google Forms, Type Forms* and *123 FormBuilder*. Create the form with questions about the topics they can talk about easily. Find out if they are experienced as podcast guests and what value they can bring to your audience. Ask for their email address, a brief bio and their social media handles. If someone is unknown to you, ensure they are a good fit for your show. Occasionally you'll encounter someone whose website looks professional but they don't speak and communicate effectively. You should ensure any guests you include have confidence in putting themselves and their ideas out there. It can be hard going as a host to have to draw answers from someone inexperienced in being interviewed.

Finally, I'm host to a free *Facebook* group where you can not only source guests, request guest interview opportunities and ask questions around podcasting, but also garner support for your release and promote your show on specific threads. Come and join us at *The Podcast Community* (*www.facebook.com/groups/ThePodcast-Community*).

Email outreach

For contacting prospective guests via email I advise creating a basic template BUT personalizing every single email you send.

Once you've set up those initial email templates (we have samples inside *The Podcast Membership*) it can take a while to get a guest booked on. For high-profile guests it can take months or until they are promoting something specific. If you don't get an immediate response, it's not necessarily a no. It's worth reaching out again with a personalized note saying why you would love to have them on. Keep a spreadsheet of who you've contacted and when, and whether they've responded or not. Keep track of how long it takes from the initial approach to recording the session as this will help you become more efficient at planning your guests and content well in advance.

Keep your request short and to the point - why you are contacting them and what it is about their work that speaks to you. I urge you again to do your research on content they have created and give a truthful account of why you enjoyed it. You have to do some due diligence here - a little bit of buttering up: what you like about their work, what you've listened to, watched, something that intrigued you, the impact their views have had on you personally. Then, describe the kind of audience you have for your podcast, the listenership figures you've achieved and why you believe your show would be a useful vehicle for them. Finally, be clear that you are open to them promoting their lead magnets, books or offers driving your audience to their email list

Make it clear that you'll be doing all you can to

increase their profile, to make it tempting to give you an hour or so of their time. This could include actions such as tags on *Instagram* or *Facebook,* social media promotions, emailing your sizeable list. Once they have agreed, ask for a brief bio and a professional headshot and send them a link to your booking calendar. Most of my interviews are done online. Occasionally I will interview in person but usually this only happens if I already have an existing relationship with the interviewee, or if I'm at an event they're attending and an impromptu interview is convenient for us both. I would ensure for recording online that they have a basic microphone set-up. At the absolute least, I'd ask that they have *Apple* earbuds (with a cable, not wireless) with them as these have a microphone embedded. Do not record with anyone who is just using their computer audio as the sound quality disparity between your microphone and theirs will be obvious. Take the lead in guiding them on acceptable equipment and expectations for the recording environment.

Scheduling

Once I've had an email confirming that the guest will come on my podcast, I send them my online booking link. I use a booking service called *Calendly*. Another to consider is *Acuity*. I send them a URL link taking them to a live booking page. This lists only the dates and times that I am available to record interviews - not my entire open calendar – and is useful as I like to record my interviews in batches on set days of the month. I book my podcast interview sessions for an hour. This doesn't mean we're recording for 60 minutes - most of my episodes are approximately 25 minutes long – but having a 60 minute session gives us ample time for the pre-interview chat, questions about the audio, any concerns they might have and a chance to build rapport before we press record. There is also time for us to have a chat afterwards and for me to tie up a few loose ends as soon as we've completed the call. Much of my work for that podcast episode is therefore done.

You can include questions on the booking form should you wish. Name, email social media handles and website links are standard. With these details in one place it's simple to copy and paste when you create show notes or social media posts later on. I usually have an option to include a weblink to a photo here, too. Since *Calendly* syncs straight into my diary, these pieces of information are easy to access prior to the call. The brief bio they provide can be used for my introduction. I make it short and snappy: who they are, what they do and who they help. It's my job to 'big them up' and make them feel appreciated, and to make sure my audience is intrigued.

A crucial question for online booking concerns intellectual property rights. Do I have permission for all of the podcast material and voice recordings to be used for promotional purposes? With my current podcast, it's compulsory for this to be answered in the affirmative for booking to proceed. Be clear that you own the audio and their voice on this recording. You never know what could become a problem down the road, and this consent will give you peace of mind. I know that some hosts require guests to sign a declaration before recording the podcast interview, which you can do using a service such as *HelloSign*. Others ask for a declaration on recorded interview before the formal questions begin - they read out a request for the guest to give full consent to use and ownership of audio. The guest replies with their name and says yes. That declaration is on record with their voice and is legally binding.

One of my final points on the booking form is an agreement to share the interview with their audience once it is published, specifically on their mailing list and each social media platform at least once. This is confirmed in an email. Of course I can never guarantee that they will share it - that's their prerogative - but if you don't ask, you don't get.

Once they have chosen a timeslot and filled in the details on my confirmation page, they receive the URL link for the *Zoom* call - my preferred platform for remote interviews. You can set up your *Calendly* system to send email and text reminders 48, 24 and one hour before your interview. Online booking systems can often be connected with Customer Relationship Manager (CRM) systems too, such as *ActiveCampaign* or *MailChimp*, making follow-up communications easier.

Using Zoom for Interviews

There are several options open to you for recording remote interviews, including video options *Zoom* and *Skype*, or audio-only such as *Zencastr*. I believe that even if it's just audio, there's real merit in seeing someone face-to-face. It helps to deepen rapport and makes for a more connected conversation. A free account on *Zoom* allows you up to 45 minutes of recording. With a premium account you can record for longer and store the interview recordings on the cloud server. Download the software onto your computer as instructed when you create an account.

Zoom automatically records the video, joint audio and the individual speakers in separate audio tracks. This is useful as, if the wifi signal is interrupted at one end of the call, the other person's audio is still intact. However, *Zoom* is focused more on video quality than audio. If you find your audio lacks quality when compared with recording solo, I recommend recording your end of the conversation with your own recording software in addition to *Zoom*. If your guest has the same functionality, ask that they do the same and send you the completed file as a .wav, therefore providing a back-up file if required. Once the call is over, save the audio track and import it into your editing software, or upload it to *Dropbox* to share with your podcast production team.

I ensure that I am in the meeting room a minute or two before the scheduled time, ready to give my full attention to my guest. At the bottom of your screen will be a panel of options - *Microphone, Video Camera, Invite, Chat* and *Record*. Check that you're both on video and that neither has a muted microphone. Access the correct microphone by clicking the arrow next to the *Microphone* icon - make sure that your USB or XLR microphone is listed and selected rather than your built-in computer microphone. When your guest arrives, unmute their microphone. Top tip - choose the setting that enables automatic recording of your meeting. There is nothing worse than completing an interview to discover you had failed to press record. Familiarize yourself with each of these functions before your first interview so that you're at ease with the software.

Pre-interview chat

The opportunity to build rapport is never stronger than at the start of your session. During these few minutes you have a chance to put your guest's mind at rest, settle into the conversation and create the foundations for an ongoing professional relationship. Through guests I have met for the first time on a *Zoom* call, I have made valuable connections, some of which have led to significant financial collaborations, others to paid speaking opportunities and several to forming close friendships with like-minded entrepreneurs. Many have become clients. Set the right tone, and you will create content that is a deep, honest and thought-provoking discussion which has meaning for both you and your guest and, mostly importantly, your listeners.

Think about how to establish rapport. How can you create that sense of ease? I like to make sure that my guest is comfortable both in the conversation and their environment … that they've got everything they need. I consider it my responsibility to bring good energy and focus. I want our interview to feel like a normal conversation. Even experienced interviewees can be a bit nervous about speaking into the microphone, particularly when they don't know you. I want them to feel that I am respectful of their time and that the time they're giving me is worthwhile. I let them know immediately that their audio sounds great if it does. That reassurance can help them to relax – another reason to wear quality headphones. You'll need to know immediately if you're getting any sound feedback or hissing during the call, or if there are any issues with their recording set-up. Occasionally, if your guest isn't using headphones or earbuds, feedback interrupts and distorts the sound. Prompt them to use earphones or headphones to prevent their sound bleeding.

Give your guest a brief description of your audience, who you're speaking to. This helps them to tailor their personal anecdotes and advice. Let them know how long you intend to be recording for and find out if they have a hard deadline. Give them the sense that you're in charge and that they can trust you to run the interview effectively. Next, check how to pronounce their name. Before you press record, remind them to double-check that all their notifications are off and that their phone is on silent or in airplane mode. Whilst you can edit out the odd accidental beep or ping (or at least an experienced audio engineer can) by recording clean audio you're making the process smoother and less time-consuming. Turning off notifications also reduces distraction. Beeps and pings make guests panic. They're worried it will ruin the interview and this can throw the conversation off course, particularly frustrating in the midst of a poignant moment or revelation.

Advise your guest to have drinking water to hand and make sure you both have a sip before you launch into the episode proper.

Before the interview you may choose to send your guest an outline of questions you will ask. I don't - I like to meet the person on *Zoom* and gain a feel for what we'll talk about. Then I tailor my questions by listening closely and responding naturally to the flow. If they prefer to know in advance, just give them a flavour of your questions. I do inform them, however, of the type of question I'll ask at the end of the interview so they'll know we're soon to finish.

I also give them the general structure of the interview including how I'll introduce them so that my listeners know who they are and why I'm excited about them coming on. I usually record this guest introduction after we have concluded the interview so that I can discuss the highlights and what I personally gained from the conversations. This helps me to tease the listener to stick around and listen in.

Before hitting record, I tell them that I'm going to go quiet for up to 30 seconds whilst I attend to the audio. It gives me a moment to get into interviewer mode and to record room tone - valuable for the editing phase. The room tone with your guest on the other end of the line is different to the room tone when you are alone in front of your recording set-up.

The shape of your interview

When I began interviewing guests on my first podcast, I was really structured. I would have 10 to 15 questions and I would ask every single one of them, regardless of the responses. That was fine as it gave me a safety net. However, doing the same interview style over again can become boring for your audience. Doggedly committing to formal questioning prevents natural conversation. And having been on the receiving end of that type of interview, I can assure you that it feels a bit uncomfortable. I suggest instead that you have maybe five questions that you can ask if the need arises, but that you allow the conversation to develop naturally.

As interviewer, you do have to be in control. When an expert dives into their own topic or story, they can become passionate … and talkative, and it can be hard to cut into them. Be an active listener. Give your guest space to share their stories and their value and do your best not to interrupt or talk over them. It is a skill that takes time to develop and is another reason I prefer to record via a video rather than an audio-only platform as it helps to judge the non-verbal cues, such as when they are concluding a tough story. Inevitably, though, you will encounter a guest who talks more than you would like. Remember that your listeners want to hear what they have to say. Let them speak until that natural pause for breath. This is your opportunity to say: 'That's really interesting. Thank you. Now I'm going to take you back to {insert earlier topic}'. You are directing the shape of the interview authoritatively whilst still allowing them space to share their views. This can be tricky if they've gone completely off tangent, but listeners want to hear your guests. They want to hear their value. They also want to hear your take on what they've said – just allow that guest to speak first.

You could influence the shape of the interview prior to recording by running through with your guest the following questions. This structure is based loosely on the *4Mat* system in *Neuro-Linguistic Programming*, designed to ensure that delivery of content appeals to all learning preferences:

What are we talking about? (An overview of the topic)
Why is it important? (What difference would this make to the listener?)
How can it be implemented? (What are the specific steps to creating the desired result?)
What if? (What if it is implemented? What if it isn't?)
When? - Usually this is about taking action now, and is

a useful segueway into including any resources such as freebies, courses, previous podcast episodes or videos you or your guest may have produced in relation to the topic.

Having a loose interview structure in mind helps to bring the conversation back on track when necessary.

I recently met Lewis Howes, host of *The School of Greatness Podcast,* one of the most popular podcasts in America. Speaking at an event he described an approach he uses to get to the heart of a conversation quickly. In his pre-interview chat he asks the guest: *What do you not want to talk about? What would be challenging for you to talk about today?* Often there will be a topic or experience that they don't want to discuss. He will probe further into why, and then say: 'Well, you know, for my audience and for you, I want to make sure that this is the most engaging interview that you've ever given. Are you sure you're not willing to go there? Because sometimes there are things that we shy away from talking about that are actually the most fascinating part of us.' Since I incorporated this into my interviews I've had some success with delving directly into the heart of a potentially challenging topic. It might be worth considering this kind of question in the pre-interview stage.

I round off my interviews with a request for my

guest to share where listeners can best connect with them, giving them ample opportunity for promotion. I thank the interviewee for their time and stop the audio recording.

Post-interview

After recording, there is another chance for a brief chat. I tell them that I thought the interview went well and which aspects I particularly enjoyed. Guests sometimes worry about not being sufficiently interesting or relevant. It is your job to put their mind at rest. Let them know they have given value.

I also like to give them a rough idea of their interview's expected release date and tell them I will be in touch about the launch with exact links to their episode and any social media images or audiograms that I may have created for them to use. I email them immediately after the interview, the day before release and the day of release.

Before we conclude the session, I ask for guest recommendations for people who may be a fit for my podcast. These have often led to email or *LinkedIn* introductions. Always close the conversation with thanks for their time and effort on behalf of your show.

After the session

Once the guest has left the online meeting room, think about how to introduce the guest and the episode. What were the chief takeaways? What surprised you about the interview? How can you build intrigue, excitement and enticement to continue listening beyond the first 60 seconds? Using the brief bio they sent, I craft an outline of the highlights of the show, building up interest in the guest and what they will share within the podcast. I record this as a short solo track to be positioned between the official podcast intro and the main interview. It introduces the guest, their value, achievements and any of my favourite moments from the interview.

File Naming

Once you close the *Zoom* meeting room, your files are made available in the 'Recordings' section of the *Zoom* website. These are in .mp3 form, ready for you to download into your software to begin editing. I save my files directly to *Dropbox* via my Mac so that they are backed up on the cloud server. Audio files can take up significant space on your hard drive and this protects my Mac from losing valuable internal disk space.

At this point, the allocated file number provided

when you download the file from *Zoom* will be a complex, long number including the date of your recording. I recommend renaming the file to include the episode number and the name of the guest followed by the episode title. From the completed interview, I may have an idea of the kind of keyword-driven title I want to use. When a file has not yet been edited, I include the label 'raw' in the file name. An example would look like this:

006_Anna Parker-Naples_How to podcast to build authority_raw.mp3

I create a folder for all of my raw tracks and a separate folder for edited tracks, in which I replace the 'raw' with the term 'final'

Be strict about file naming. Effective file naming at this stage makes it easier to pull those files into *Audacity* or whichever editing software you use. You'll be able to distinguish which audio track is which when working on multiple tracks.

Guest Emails

Create a template of your follow-up emails and add in episode-specific details. Include one email immediately after the interview thanking them for their time and expertise, another to send the day before the episode goes live reminding them that they promised to share the interview with their audience and a third including all of the links to the episode upon release, including your social media handles for maximizing the chance of your show reaching their audience's ears.

Guest relationships

One of the hidden benefits of podcasting is the potential for return on investment of your time and crafting your podcast through developing high-level relationships with other experts. By strategizing who you invite onto your show, you can build and strengthen real and meaningful collaboration opportunities. It is not uncommon for even your guest becoming a client if you have an offer that is appealing to them.

In this chapter I've covered everything you need to get started with recording your show. Once you've created valuable content that has the ability to inspire, motivate and engage your audience, it's time to make it sound amazing in the editing process.

Podcast Spotlight

Nicola Huelin, *Mpower podcast for mums in business - Bounce Back Interview series*

2020 was a tough year for most people around the world and the podcast. Sharing inspirational stories and secrets of how other mums have bounced back from tough times and periods of adversity was part of my personal mission to help as many women as possible bounce back from the challenges of 2020 and bounce forward into 2021 even stronger.

Since launching our podcast, we reached #2 in the *iTunes* charts, *Top Shows in Business*, topping business podcasting greats including Gary Vee and Tony Robbins. The show received 58 5 star reviews within the first week alone. Combining the podcast chart success and the results of a national *Bounce Back* survey I ran in collaboration with *Chocolate PR* and insurance company *Bounce*, *Mpower* has had lots of feature articles in the media. I've also been able to interview lots of amazing people including ex-Atomic Kitten superstar Natasha Hamilton and Emmerdale actress Natalie Anderson.

I'd already launched an initial podcast series two years prior, but as it was research for my book I was happy to launch it organically. This time, having a podcast sponsor and wanting to ensure we had some PR worthy launch results, I really wanted to make sure I had the best launch strategy possible. I had a strategy consultation with Anna which really helped me validate my chosen launch strategy, identify some blind spots and get my outstanding questions answered.

Anna's feedback and insights meant I could feel 100% confident that I was launching the podcast in the best way possible to achieve my aims of getting into the charts in order to generate some great PR input. As a strategist myself I know the difference it makes when you can put your time, energy and money behind a strategy you know is the right one and will get results.

Podcasting gives me an incredible platform to connect with amazing people, increases the visibility of *Mpower*, contributes to my mission to empower one million mums in business, highlights the vision and values behind my work as one of the UK's leading business mentors and marketing strategists for mums in business and creates inspirational, value-adding content to share with the *Mpower* community and my wider network.

For someone looking to start a podcast I

would advise you to know your audience, give them value, be clear on what you want your podcast to achieve for your audience and your business, be authentic, have a plan, get support to learn the bits you don't know how to do and enjoy the process.

9

EDITING

Editing used to put the fear of God into me. I was petrified that I would get it wrong and be found out in some way as a total fraud. In my previous work as a voice actor there were two camps - those from a performance background and those from an audio engineering or radio background who relished the technology. Needless to say, I was in the first camp. I had little interest in audio editing and was a bit scared of the technical stuff. When I ventured into recording and editing from home I looked for ways to minimize and simplify the process.

Having produced and edited thousands of hours of audio in all genres, I now realize that audio editing procedures CAN be complex and are particularly necessary if you are creating broadcast quality or *Dolby* surround sound. The level and depth to which you concern yourself with advanced and sophisticated mixing and mastering processes depends on the aims of your podcast. A professionally-produced show will stand out. Decide how much having that premier feel about your podcast matters to you and your personal brand. If it IS paramount, work with a podcast production agency to ensure you create a supreme audio product. My agency works with tons of podcast hosts who want premium level quality with a total *done-for-them* package. This allows them to focus on delivering content and growing their business.

Not everyone has the same drivers for their podcast, and it is ALWAYS better to get started than to procrastinate. Podcasts are predominantly listened to through iPhones and smart speakers. The files are compressed in order to be uploaded into the podcast host and compressed again by the likes of *Apple*. So yes, undeniably audio quality is vital. However, it is far more important to get your podcast started and improve as you go. If you wait until your editing abilities are perfect you will never get going. If you can't afford to work with a professional production team, then just begin. It takes many hours of practice to achieve perfection. Editing my first 19-hour-long audiobook was a baptism of fire. You can refine and improve your processes later.

In this chapter I will share what I consider to be

achievable by anyone with the ability to highlight, copy and paste. There are, of course, many processes that would enhance your audio and if this is an area you choose to develop your skills in, then you will have a solid foundation and understanding upon which to draw.

However, there is a limit to how much I can share about editing with the written word. If you need more detailed, visual teachings visit *www.ThePodcastMembership.com*. For simplicity, I will focus on the free *Audacity* programme since it is almost identical on both Macs and PC's. This section is intended to give you an overview that is 'good enough'. It is not intended to teach you full mixing and mastering at advanced levels, much of which is achieved only after years of experience.

Editing is essentially how you enhance the raw audio to make it sound better - richer, error-free and easier to listen to. It is the part of the audio process where you can bring separate elements of your recordings together - music, intro, outro and the main body of the show - and then export the mixed file ready to upload onto a podcast hosting platform.

The basic functions inside *Audacity* are similar to those in any editing software. You will recognize the main buttons: *pause, play, stop, record, skip forward* and *back*. These are the most used functions when recording and editing.

If recording directly into the software, make sure that the correct microphone is selected. Ensure that your closed back headphones are selected in the speaker setting rather than your computer's inbuilt speakers. I hope I've stressed enough that it is imperative you use these for hearing the imperfections in your audio tracks as you edit.

To start a new track you can choose between mono or stereo recordings. When I'm recording voice-only, I tend to record in mono. To import a track that you have pre-recorded - for example, the 'raw' file you created when you recorded via *Zoom* - click on *File*, then *Import.*

Basic editing tools

Selection tool – This is the one you'll use most. It allows you to highlight specific areas to edit in one go.

Envelope tool – This allows you to increase and decrease volume to fade in and out at particular points, for example when you fade the music track behind your voice track as you begin the main body of your podcast content.

Cut tool - The cut tool is one of the most important early-stage tools for copying and pasting. It looks like a knife.

Zoom tool - The magnifying glass icon is fairly self-explanatory. You can zoom in and out on various parts of the audio on the waveform to examine it for more detailed editing work. This can be useful for close work when removing loud breath sounds like 'ums' and 'ahs'.

Time Shift tool – This allows you to highlight sections of audio that you wish to position at a different timed location, useful when combining several tracks into one.

Undo & redo buttons - You'll be familiar with these from any *Word* or *Excel* document. They can be a godsend if you are overly keen with your editing as they enable you to quickly amend your work.

To get started, press record and do a quick test on your connected microphone. As you speak you'll see the visuals on the waveform move up and down on a panel with yellow and red levels on a bar. Make sure your audio does not go into the red zone on the bar as that means it is 'peaking' - best to avoid as it is challenging to repair the distortion. To prevent this (depending on the make and model) you may be able to adjust the 'gain' directly on your microphone. If not possible, the level of sound received by your microphone can be adjusted on your audio interface or directly in *Audacity*.

Next to the speaker icon is a slider showing the speed at which the audio is played back to you. There is an option to increase or decrease the playback speed. Once you've completed the first edit to remove basic errors and noises you might not want to listen to the whole episode in real-time, but at a faster speed. However, you MUST listen at least once to the entire track at real-time speed during the edit in order to be aware of the listener experience.

Noise Reduction process

In the recording chapter I mentioned the importance of having 30 seconds of background room tone recorded before you (and your guest) begin speaking. In *Audacity* there is a facility for removing the majority of the room tone background noises in one go. To do this, highlight the blank 30 seconds of room tone and in the menu at the top of the screen select *Noise Removal* in the *Effects* tab. Click to open the *noise removal* tool. Room tone is not the same as silence, however indiscernible the difference might be to your naked ear. Press to get *Noise Profile* then go back and highlight the entire length of the track. Go to *Effect, Noise Reduction*. This time you can select what degree of noise you want removed, which will depend entirely on your recording space and how noisy the background is. Test out different options between level 12 and 18. Click 'OK'.

The entire length of the track has now been

treated. It won't make much of a difference to the waveforms visually but you'll be able to hear the change through your headphones.

The next part of the process is to listen to the whole track for pops, clicks and speech stumbles - where maybe you've said something incorrectly, repeated yourself or used excessive um's, ah's or long pauses as you consider what to say next. With practice you'll become efficient at spotting these in the audio. To remove any sections you don't want to include, highlight and then delete.

How much of the breaths, umms and ahs you remove is a stylistic choice. Sometimes it is preferable to quieten the breath sound rather than delete it completely so that the natural pacing and rhythm of the speech is maintained.

Listen out for lip smacks, wet mouth sounds and deep breaths. When interviewing, I like to create that fly on the wall feeling in the audio. Others might opt for a sleeker, polished and crisp sound.

Once you have worked on the voice-only recording you can import the music track and audio for your intro. All imported tracks are displayed on the panel, one under the other. With the time shift tool you can lay them out in order for when each track will start. You can then decide where you want to fade the music and voice sections in and out.

With all elements of your track on screen, you can see it in its entirety. See how you can improve its overall sound. There are many different ways to do this and I've learned from 15 years of audio experience that there is no single correct way. Many of those processes are over-complicated for an entry level podcast and certainly too complex to go over in this book. However, if you want your show to sound the best it can be, work with a production team that knows how to make your audio sound excellent.

When satisfied with the shape and overall quality of the file, click 'Select All' and in *Effects* click 'Normalise'. This helps to balance out the volume levels of the track. You may want to compress the track or add EQ as part of the mastering of your audio. These are advanced editing techniques - if you're not ready to outsource, play around and explore how these processes and effects make your track sound. We have further trainings inside *The Podcast Membership*.

Here are some terms to familiarize yourself with:

Mastering is the final step of audio post-production. The purpose of mastering is to balance sonic elements of a mix of tracks and optimize playback across all systems and media formats. Traditionally, mastering is done using tools like equalization, compression, limiting and stereo enhancement. Think of mastering as the glue, varnish and polish that optimizes playback quality on all devices from tiny *iPhone* speakers to massive dance club sound systems. Mastering bridges the gap between artist (in this case podcaster!) and consumer. The term itself comes from the idea of a master copy. Additionally, mastering allows for restoration of hisses, clicks or small mistakes missed in the final mix. Mastering ensures uniformity and consistency of sound between multiple tracks.

Ultimately, mastering creates a clean and cohesive feeling across all your audio.

Compression is the process of reducing the dynamic range between the loudest and quietest parts of an audio signal. This is done by boosting the quieter signals and attenuating (reducing) the louder signals.

Equalization - EQ for short - means boosting or reducing (attenuating) the levels of different frequencies in a signal. Equalization is most commonly used to correct signals that sound unnatural. For example, if a sound was recorded in a room which accentuates high frequencies, an equalizer can reduce those frequencies to a more normal level. Equalization can also be used to make sounds more intelligible and reduce feedback.

Exporting your file

When you have finished editing the track, export the audio as a .mp3 file - the required audio specification for *Apple* and *Spotify*. At this point you'll be given options for choosing the bit rate. 16 bit is sufficient for voice recordings. Export as a .mp3, selecting 44.1 kHz or 41000 Hz and 128 or 192kbps if you are given the options. Whichever you go for, be consistent across all of your files. Occasionally with *Audacity*, particularly on some older style PCs, the option to export to .mp3 won't be available. If this is the case you will need to download a *LAME* code. Google will be your friend for this. After completing your first finished track, save the set-up as a project template. Most of your episodes will follow an identical structure and this will save you hours of time in the long run.

Editing can be as complex or as simple as you make it. I promise that you'll learn a great deal through practice, listening and more practice. Don't be overwhelmed. If you realize early on that this is not an area you want to focus your time on, find an experienced podcast editor to outsource to. This doesn't have to be a headache for you. We have a full podcast production agency that can take care of all technical aspects of your show.

Adding Metadata tags to .mp3 files

I wish I had known the value of tagging when I launched my first podcast. Tags can be added to your completed .mp3 audio track and are effectively attached to the audio wherever it goes, a little like a tattoo. You can include information on ownership, a description of the audio and even a mini bio of your specific episode. This is useful because each podcast directory reads the audio files in a unique way. If tags are embedded at this stage in the proceedings, you are giving your audio, and hence your podcast, the best chance of appearing in keyword searches in each of the hundreds of podcast directories in the marketplace. This metadata makes you and your show much more likely to appear in searches.

In some podcast hosting platforms such as *Libsyn* (which we'll look at in detail in the next chapter) you have the option to add tags directly within the site. I would recommend using a specific software such as *ID3 Editor* as it allows for greater levels of depth and detail. This is available from *pa-software.com* and after tagging your first .mp3 you can create a template to streamline the process going forward.

Now that your track is edited and tagged it's time to prepare to upload it, get your show on the road and out into the big wide world. You're almost there.

Podcast Spotlight

Nikki Collinson-Phenix, *The Profitable Couch*

I started my podcast for two reasons:

1. I had always dreamed of having my own radio show - I just didn't tell anyone. I mean, I have had this dream since I was little. I loved being asked to be a guest on the radio and just felt comfortable when I was on there, totally at home and saddened when it was over. I told myself one day I would have my own show, I just didn't know how it would look. As I got older and started listening to podcasts, I wondered if this was a path I could take one day.

2. As the effects of Covid-19 hit my industry, I could see my fellow health and wellness professionals confused, lost and without direction. I had been mentoring them on the business side of therapy for around 18 months through my community *The Profitable Couch* and it broke my heart to see my whole community battered by what was happening. I had to close the doors to my treatment room and so I knew how they were feeling. I knew

they were looking to me for guidance, support, advice and leadership. I knew in that moment that I had to step up more than I had ever done and give them as much support as I could. I, too, was holed up at home, juggling homeschooling and navigating my business. Many of these incredible therapists had assumed that because they could not be in the treatment room, their businesses were closed. I wanted to show them that it was only their treatment rooms that were closed, not their businesses! Their businesses were OPEN and their clients/patients still needed their help and guidance. I wanted to show them that they could still provide guidance, advice and support to them, just in a different way. I wanted them to learn to focus on what they COULD do and not what they couldn't do. I felt so passionate about helping every one of them navigate these challenging times. So I sat and tried to work out how I could help them from my attic, how could I reach as many of my fellow health and wellness professionals in a way that felt right and felt comfortable and there came the idea to launch the podcast. I didn't need a fancy set-up. I didn't need hair and make-up. I just needed a voice, a message, a mic, some headphones and the internet. There was nothing stopping me from helping my tribe. As a recovering perfectionist, this would be imperfect action in all its glory, doing everything I could to positively impact those in my world who needed that help. My mantra was 'wherever you can listen, you can learn' And so the journey began ....

Since the launch it's been an amazing rollercoaster ride! Seeing my podcast hit #2 in the charts for *Entrepreneurship* just pipped by the likes of Tim Ferris, and above names like Tony Robbins, Carrie Green, Gary Vaynerchuk to name a few, was like a dream come true! I have had such incredible feedback and I love it when one of my community members posts that they've been for a walk listening to one of the episodes and had a massive business breakthrough. My audience continues to grow and the podcast now has a structure and a place in the impactful work that I do. I have been approached regarding sponsorship, although I am yet to step in that direction, and I am learning how to repurpose the content. My visibility has grown as has my position as an expert in my field. I am so, so glad I launched it! The future is now full of so much possibility.

Anna came into my world at an epically crucial time in my podcast. I was sat in my attic office basking in my imperfect action having just uploaded my first episode to *iTunes* that evening. I had just wanted to upload an episode, to walk myself through the process and see 'how to do it'! I posted in a group the next day that I was celebrating a win by uploading this episode and Anna replied to congratulate me and I can't remember the words but it was something along the lines of now being in launch mode! I was really confused as I wasn't yet ready to 'launch' … I was just testing the waters … so I watched a training she had done a few months back and had a massive awakening that by releasing that first episode I was now indeed in a launch and that I had a two-week window to maximise its visibility. Oh f**k, that imperfect action didn't feel so great then! Ha Ha! I went over to my husband and said: 'It appears I am now in a launch, see you in two weeks!' I went back up to my attic, joined Anna's membership and worked my socks off for the next fortnight. Anna was always checking in with me on how it was going and watching my progress as I went head first 0-100mph into launch mode. She would check the charts with me and give me a boost when I was having a wobble! I binge-watched her training and I just knew that she had my back.

If Anna had not commented on my post it would never have triggered me to delve further into what she meant about 'launch mode' when it came to the podcast. I would have missed a key crucial window of opportunity and the podcast would have probably never even got near the charts let alone #2. I am so happy I took that imperfect action, and I truly worked my socks off those two weeks. It was exhausting, exciting, draining and an adrenaline rush, but none of it would have happened if Anna hadn't crossed my path at that crucial time.

My audience continues to grow and continues to assist me in giving me credibility in my industry. It has also helped my imposter syndrome no end! And it has allowed me to give those who can't yet afford to work with me access to help - so I also see it as part of my funnel. I am in the process of learning how to repurpose better so it will help me massively with my content moving forward.

If you are considering starting a podcast, my advice is just do it!

If you have a message to share that could help someone then you need to get that message out there. It does not need to be perfect. It just needs to be real.

Don't let tech hold you back. If you don't want to do it yourself then outsource.

Connect and learn from those who have gone before you to save time and costly mistakes

Make sure you have an audience ready to hear your podcast. They will be the ones you need to help you get it the visibility it deserves.

Have fun with it and just enjoy yourself!

10

HOSTING

One of the first questions I'm asked by aspiring podcasters is 'How do you get your show on *iTunes?*' The answer is through a podcast hosting platform. This is essentially the home of your podcast, where the audio is uploaded and stored together with all the accompanying details required by individual podcast directories. Through a *RSS* feed the content is then pushed out to the major podcast directories if you have created an account with them. RSS stands for "Rich Site Syndication" or "Really Simple Syndication." Put simply, an RSS feed is a script that people can subscribe to in order to access updates to online content, such as a blog or podcast. A podcast RSS feed is what allows users to subscribe to that podcast in order to listen to it without visiting the exact website where it is located. It also updates subscribers when new episodes are uploaded, so they never have to go searching for them.

There are various podcast hosting platforms to choose from, with assorted levels of functionality, cost and ease of use. These include *Podbean*, *Spreaker*, *Buzz-Sprout*, *Anchor*, *Captivate* and *Libsyn*, to name just a few platforms in this rapidly developing area. As the podcast industry expands many new hosts are appearing, many of which are free. Some established podcasters are wary of utilizing these platforms. Although they make it extremely straightforward to publish your podcast they are free because you effectively hand over your rights to controlling the adverts placed on your podcast at a later date. As the free platforms grow and seek to monetize their service they will exert their right to place paid adverts anywhere in your content. The ads will not have been curated for your audience and this can be the biggest turn-off for your listeners.

The platform that I use and recommend is *Libsyn*. It has been the longest-running service and is amongst the most reliable platforms around. The monthly subscription starts at $5 – enough to get your show up and running. If you require more detailed, advanced statistics or want to batch record and upload several months' worth of podcast episodes in one go, you can upgrade or downgrade your plan at any point. If you're just getting going in the online business world an advantage of Libsyn is that they create a website extension for your podcast that you can personalize to a small degree. I don't use it myself because part of my podcasting strategy is to drive people to my own website where I can capture their information through cookies or lead magnets and opt-in boxes. If you don't have your own website yet, what *Libsyn* offers even in the basic package is good enough for your show to have a home on the internet.

After selecting your plan in *Libsyn* you'll be directed to create a 'Show Slug'. The *slug* is a unique name that is associated with your show and makes up your show URLs. I would advise you to use the name of your podcast and be aware that the slug is the one section of your podcast that you cannot change. The 'Show Slug' informs the RSS Feed, which is how all the information gets pushed out to the podcast directories. It also makes up part of the *Libsyn* website domain name, e.g. *www.EntrepreneursGetVisible.Libsyn.com*.

Once you have registered a new show visit the *Settings* tab and complete the relevant details. These would include the Show Settings with your important keyword-rich description and show title, the podcast host's name, the copyright notice and the main artwork for your podcast. Select content categories you'd like your show to be positioned in. This will influence how *iTunes* and *Spotify* list your podcast and the charts you may (or may not) be listed in when you launch. You are allowed to select three. Getting this right is essential for an effective launch. In the *Settings* section you can add brand-consistent colours and presets for all of your episodes. These include labelling your content as clean, explicit or not set. As the major players in the industry make in-roads in protecting young ears from hearing unsuitable language, I urge you to set this appropriately. The last thing you want is for *iTunes* or *Google* to give your show a red flag and limit your reach.

The *Content* tab is where you can find any previously published episodes and any that you have in draft before they are released. This is where you will upload your first episode and all of the corresponding details including the imagery, media file (your edited .mp3) and episode-specific details. These are, in essence, abbreviated show notes into which you can place weblinks you wish to direct your listeners towards.

One of the main benefits of *Libsyn* is that once you have set up with the major podcast players your show can be connected to many smaller platforms at the push of a button and your episodes automatically released onto your social platforms should you wish. It is worth adding your podcast to as many platforms as possible. It costs nothing and if you are spending time and effort putting your show together why not ensure it can be found wherever someone may be choosing to tune in?

You can also schedule the release of your episodes. It pays to be consistent with the days and times that you publish as fans of your show will know when to look out for your next episode in their podcast feed. My episodes are released at 5.30am on a Monday and Thursday. This gives time for them to be picked up by the major players before my emails and social media announce to the world that the new episode is live. I pick Monday because many of my listeners want to begin their week inspired and many have jobs that involve a commute. The timings work for my listenership and for me.

When you have scheduled your first episode, your podcast is almost ready to submit to *iTunes*.

Validating Your Feed

Apple Podcasts is still the most popular podcast platform but there may be hurdles to overcome in getting your show submitted. I recommend having your RSS feed validated using an online checking system before you attempt to upload it onto *Apple*. Errors on your RSS feed can cause considerable delays and difficulties in re-submitting your show. Once you've completed the basic show set-up in *Libsyn* and released one episode on the platform, copy the link to the RSS feed and paste it into a site such as *castfeedvalidator.com*. It takes less than a minute to run basic tests and displays any issues with the podcast. The most common problems are incorrectly uploading a media file or an artwork file being the incorrect size.

Submitting to *iTunes*

For getting your podcast on *iTunes* you need an *Apple iTunes* account. With your *Apple* ID, go to *iTunes Connect* which you can easily find through a search in *Google*. You will see a dashboard and a tab named 'Podcast Connect'. From here you can add a new podcast using the RSS code you copied from *Libsyn*. Then click 'Validate'. If all looks good and no warning issues are displayed click 'Submit'.

You will receive an email confirming submission of your show and that it is being reviewed. It can take anything from 24 hours to seven days for this to happen – a challenge for your launch strategy. Be aware, too, that you won't always receive a confirmation email to inform you that your show is live. Check *iTunes* on a daily basis to see if you can find your show title and your name in a search. As soon as your show is live in *iTunes*, get promoting. Don't wait until it is on all platforms - the *iTunes* charts begin monitoring a new show's download activity immediately.

Submitting to *Spotify, Stitcher & Google*

Spotify are ploughing tons of investment capital into podcasts, with plans to dominate the industry. As I write this they have unveiled their first chart system for all podcast listens across their platform.

It may be that your *Libsyn* account is automatically releasing content to *Spotify*. Check in the *Destinations* tab … if not, sign up for an account at *www.podcasters.spotify.com* and claim your podcast. *Spotify* are working fast to increase the level and depth of statistics around podcast downloads and are well-placed to pool together detailed information around the gender, location, interests and other demographics. Keep abreast of the developments they make. It can take a few weeks for *Spotify* to accept your podcast, and is not guaranteed.

Get your show hosted by *Stitcher*. You have to apply to be listed with them, and there is a heavy vetting system. They require your show to be live before you apply, and audio quality is crucial. Search for the *Stitcher Partner Portal* and make an application once your show is published elsewhere.

Finally, visit the podcast portal in *Google Podcasts*.

Again, this is by application only and will not happen immediately. In some countries it is not yet possible to apply. Changes are being made rapidly in the podcast industry so check back and try again in a few months. Likewise, *Amazon* and *Audible* are entering the podcast market so watch out for opportunities to submit your podcast there, too.

Once you are listed on the main directories, return to the *Libsyn Destination* tab and connect to each of the smaller directories that are listed. New directories crop up all the time - some derive their information from other platforms and others require an application. Look out for the latest directories every few months.

Podcast Spotlight

Andy Lopata, *The Connected Leadership Podcast*

I had a number of reasons to launch this podcast. I have published two previous podcast series and it was always in the back of my mind but the impetus was the need to reposition my business and offer both as part of a wider strategy - driven by the lockdown because of the Covid-19 Pandemic.

My primary objectives are to give my

current network greater insight into what I am doing, strengthen my positioning in the leadership space and to attract new followers and clients. The podcast ties in between the publication of two new books and is designed to work with those to take my business to the next part of its journey.

In addition, I have an amazing network with people who have fantastic experiences others can learn from. I'm in a privileged position to be able to bring those stories to the fore and the podcast is a great way to achieve that.

My previous two attempts at podcasting had limited impact because I lacked any strategy behind the podcasts. While I had grasped the basics, Anna's support has given me that strategic thinking, meaning that I have made core changes to approach, editing, format and more. I have also upped my technical game thanks to Anna's ideas and feedback.

I have spent more time analyzing other podcasts, thinking about my audience, looking at marketing techniques and more than I would have done otherwise.

If I had not had this support the

consequence would have been fewer listeners, less engaging shows, poorer technical quality and much less impact. I would probably have been in the same place as before, adequate and interesting shows shared with a small community for a short period of time before getting disgruntled and moving on to the next idea.

My advice for anyone considering starting a podcast is this - don't rush it. Be strategic, do your research, plan everything carefully and hit the ground running. I recommend Anna's membership to everyone I speak to who is thinking of launching a podcast. The resources are fantastic and the community is a great support, too.

11

SHOW NOTES & WEBSITES

Making your podcast work for you

In this chapter we'll look at how to use show notes to enhance your podcast and give you more online reach and longevity. As with other areas of podcasting there are no fixed guidelines. What you choose to do, or not do, with your show notes is entirely up to you.

Show notes are the text you upload in the description section on *Libsyn* for each episode and the text that potential listeners view before clicking on your episode. More commonly, when podcast hosts mention show notes they are referring to the information connected to the podcast that is housed on their website. Each show note page is effectively a blogpost including an image, an audio player with that specific episode, the title and a description of the episode. Often it includes links to further resources or episodes that relate to the episode, more guest information and their weblink and social media handles ... and, crucially, an opt-in form to join the podcast host's mailing list.

The benefits of creating show notes are manifold. They enable a quick decision to listen to the show or not. They signpost the listener to further resources and content relevant to the episode. Additionally, they are useful for funneling listeners into your mailing list, paid products and services or to affiliate links of someone else's services. Finally, you have the option to include your podcast episodes on your website. The benefit of this is that they provide valuable opportunities to improve your SEO by giving you new, relevant and regular published content to build your domain authority as a long-term strategy.

For listeners who are time-poor, show notes enable them to scan the accompanying text for the main points made in the show. You can include timestamps to specific moments in the episode when a particular piece of information was discussed. Some podcast players allow these timestamps to be created automatically for you, e.g. *Fusebox.com* and *Searchie.io*.

When I set up my first podcast I had no show notes at all. Gradually I began to include a brief synopsis of my guest and the topic we were covering. I added this in only to the description on *Libsyn*. I did not include it on my website. When I began to embed the episodes on my website, I included no details about the show beyond the title. Now I am much more targeted for results in my business. The reason for describing my own evolution is so that you see how you can do as little or as much as you want. It depends on the results you want for your show. As a bare minimum, by using *Libsyn* you will have a podcast website to direct people to.

For the episode description preferences vary from none at all, to brief bullet points, to full length transcripts of the entire episode. If you're considering using full transcriptions there are services such as *Otter.ai* for transcribing your podcast audio for free. Other options are *rev.com* and *descript.com*. Although transcription services are fairly accurate (and some such as *Searchie.io* and *Otter.ai* are responsive to the corrections you make with the ability to transcribe to your preferences in future) you should do a full edit check for grammar, spelling and any general punctuation. When we speak we don't converse technically correctly. I have a naturally quick tempo and find that a lot of my sentences blur together in transcribed text. If you have short episodes it may be worth considering a full transcript, but if your podcasts are an hour or more in length it would be a sizeable task to edit each full transcription.

Creating Show Notes

You can speed up the process of creating show notes by considering, before recording, the general shape, outcomes and resources you'll mention during your episode. You could include what you want listeners to take away from the episode, why they'd listen. Make a list of the topics you'll be covering. Create this as a template in *Word* and for each episode so that your show notes are already outlined. Having this outline makes it easy to come back to the focus on the key takeaways should I go off on a tangent. During the episode, a book may be mentioned. After recording I add that book as an additional resource to the episode outline. Once I have reviewed my show notes to ensure everything is included and relevant, I copy them to the description on *Libsyn* and to a draft version of the blog-post I will create for that episode. I read over the topics I've covered and do some keyword research for SEO to ensure I am making the most effective choices for building search engine authority.

From a visual perspective it is also worth high-lighting on the show notes any compelling quotes. These might entice visitors to read on and can be turned into meme-style quotes for social media when it comes to your episode promotion.

I hope I have persuaded you that a podcast offers

so much potential for community, engagement and interactive action with you as the key person of influence and authority. If you constantly provide valuable content on your website, in written and audio format, you will drive people towards you, your business and your products and services. You will be positioned as a key person of influence.

Websites

The content you put on your website is fundamental to driving traffic to it. Think about how to get more of the keywords your business is associated with onto your website. This is where the show notes page for your podcast comes into play. It is the long game, though. It can take six to 12 months for *Google, Bing, Yahoo!* and other search engines to notice the quality and consistency of your content.

At the beginning of this book we looked at what you want your podcast to do for you long-term. Go further with that. What do you want to be known for? Which keywords need to be visible on your website and any material associated with the podcast?

When you launch your podcast, I advise you to share the links to *iTunes* and *Spotify* with your audience. This will drive activity to those platforms and maximize your chance of entering the charts - giving your podcast long-lasting kudos. After that period, encourage people to listen on the podcast pages of your website. This will increase awareness of your work and the possibility of a listener browsing through more of your content, opting in to one of your lead magnets or freebies in exchange for an email address or for you to capture their data via cookies, allowing you to retarget them through *Facebook* ads or similar.

With a home for your podcast on your website it is easier to promote your services, provide details of podcast sponsors (should you choose to monetize in this way) and to house an entire resource library of links and content mentioned on your show.

You could create a podcast-specific website or add a podcast section to your existing company or personal brand website. With my current podcast, I drive all listeners to *www.AnnaParkerNaples.co.uk/Podcast*. I also own the domain *www.EntrepreneursGetVisible.com* which redirects to my main site.

I want people to land on my website so that they discover further ways to work with me or explore my content and the 'Podcast' tab on my website is home to all of the show notes.

Earlier, we saw that *Libsyn* has a facility for you to have a basic website for your podcast included in your subscription. It isn't perfect, but it does the job. However, it won't help to increase your own SEO domain authority or enable you to upsell or collect listener details. When the time comes to move over to another custom-designed site, I recommend using a *Wordpress.org* based site with a theme builder. I discuss several options that are easy to use inside *The Podcast Membership*.

Throughout this book I've encouraged having strong *Call To Actions* (CTA) throughout your podcast, particularly in your outro. My current CTA is to send listeners to a page called *Get Visible* which houses a full player of my podcast together with links to many of my services that I wish to promote and several opt-ins for free content, such as checklists and how-to guides. It also enables access to the free *Facebook* group community that supports the podcast. This page is designed to help bring people into my business and is one avenue for me to monetize the podcast, with several ways to capture their details and bring them into the community.

Podcast Audio Players

When I was running my first podcast I would copy an episode-specific embed code from *Libsyn* and paste it in as a custom .html embed code onto my website so that the audio player for the specific episode would be displayed. Alternatively, if you have a *Wordpress* website you could install a *Libsyn* plugin to make it easier to add the audio onto your site. You can alter the colours and images on the audio player to fit your website branding by adjusting them within the *Libsyn* Content section. Another *Wordpress* plugin option to consider is *Simple Podcast Press*. It allows you to automatically create a separate page/blogpost for each individual episode upon release. It displays, with no further input from you, the artwork, show title, audio player and full show notes.

I'm currently using a much more advanced podcast player called *Fusebox* (previously known as *Smart Podcast Player*). The reason I decided to go with this player is its functionality. It allows listeners to scroll through and search my previous episodes. It can also display a master panel of my podcasts which I can customize to include my show notes. It comes with an option to have the current episode of the podcast displayed at the top or bottom of my website in a ribbon format.

The *Fusebox* player allows you to simply add links to each of the main directories - *iTunes*, *Spotify* and *Google* - and crucially provides easy links for sharing episodes on social media. If you don't want to create separate pages of show notes on your website this player would be more than sufficient to simplify the process. It also includes timestamps which make it easy for a website visitor to navigate to exactly the part of your episode that interests them.

To find website, show notes and podcast player styles that you like, visit the websites of the shows you have researched. Notice which website pages they are driving you towards, what affiliate links they are using, what resources they are promoting. Notice whether they host in-person events, live podcast recordings. Have they created a *Facebook* or other online community for listeners? Consider how you can best create a home for your podcast. A website is never complete and you should allow yourself to just get started and refine later.

Compiling show notes can take up a considerable amount of time and is simple to outsource. A good podcast production agency will offer this as part of their service or you could employ the services of a virtual assistant. We make the ones we create for our clients fully researched and search engine-optimized. To find out more about the full service package to edit, master, host and create show notes that my podcast production agency provides go to *www.annaparkernaples.-co.uk/podcast-production.*

Podcast Spotlight

Lori Latimer, *Grief With Grace For Grieving Moms*

I started my podcast to offer hope and inspiration to moms who have children in Heaven/Spirit so they can continue living their lives in a way that honors their late child's life and legacy. I wanted to create a community and be seen as an expert as I build a business helping these moms.

In less than two months I've released 12 episodes and have had over 1,400 downloads of my podcast. I have listeners on every continent (well, except Antarctica). My *Facebook* group is growing. Even people who aren't moms or who don't have a child in Heaven are listening and telling me how much it's impacting and helping them.

I would never have launched without Anna's membership. It gave me the steps I needed in a way that even I, as a very non-techy person, could understand and implement. The worksheets and checklists are invaluable.

If I had not had this support I literally wouldn't have ever launched my podcast.

The impact podcasting has had on me and my business has been huge. I have women reaching out to me to work with me as private clients and to join my *Facebook* group. I have people asking to be a guest on my show and I'm starting to be a guest on other people's podcasts as well. I'm creating a brand.

My advice to someone looking to start a podcast?

Follow the steps that Anna lays out. Set a launch date, put together a launch team, have a few episodes to launch with … and do it.

12

LAUNCH YOUR PODCAST

Launching your podcast with an intentional strategy gives you the best chance of success. It increases your chances of appearing in the *iTunes* and *Spotify* *Top Charts*, *New Shows* and *New & Noteworthy* sections. The longer you are listed in these sections, the more likely new listeners will discover your show. The more listeners you have, the more you can build a community and increase revenue with sales.

I launched my first podcast by just releasing it on *iTunes* and not telling anyone about it for the first few weeks. I launched my second with a full campaign, attention, effort and gusto. You can guess which one achieved stellar results and which was unspectacular. Promise me that after all the effort you've gone to in creating your podcast, you won't miss this one-time opportunity to promote your show like your life depends on it.

On the day you launch the podcast (the day *iTunes* has published your show and you can find it using the search function) you have a short window in which to achieve as many downloads, reviews, ratings and subscribers as you can. Induce as many friends, family, neighbours, colleagues, peers, followers, connections and that girl you used to go to school with – ANYONE who will take action - to help put your show on the map.

This is all made much easier if you use the eight weeks prior to launch day to build anticipation and interest in your podcast. Talk about it in your social media posts. Mention it in emails. Ask for feedback on logos, names, artwork. Ask for suggestions for guests and topics. Not only will this induce desire for your show, it will build goodwill towards your project. By the time it goes live many people will feel a part of its creation and want to see it do well.

Technically, your podcast can go live with one single audio track, preferably your trailer episode, labelled '00'. However, since the aim of your launch is to receive as many downloads as possible, you should launch at least two more episodes that day. This will make it more likely that new listeners will subscribe to your show. They will have heard enough content to judge if it is to their liking and want it to be downloaded into their podcast feed every time you release material. As a minimum, have three episodes ready to go. I also consider having a bank of content recorded and ready for release later that week so that you can continue to drive more downloads in those early days of launch. A full month and a half of prepped, finished material will give you the best head start.

When asking people to help you in your social media and personal messaging, ask them to '*Subscribe, Rate, Review & Download*' if they are listening on an *Apple* device, and to *Subscribe and Listen* on *Android* platforms such as *Google, Spotify and Stitcher.*

The most effective launches are well planned and given time, effort and attention for at least the first week of launch, much as you would with the launch of any product or service. A challenge with this is that you have no control over when *iTunes* will release your show once you have submitted the RSS feed for validation. It could be anywhere between 24 hours to seven days. I would advise to have as much of your social media planned, images created and emails drafted – be ready to go as soon as you have notification that your show is live. The more prepared you are, the less you will feel as though you are scrabbling to keep up with a busy launch period. Once your show starts climbing the charts do not let it slip until you have pushed it as far up as you can get it!

Encourage support for your launch

One option to consider in order to increase your chances of people supporting your podcast launch at the time you want them to take action is to host an event, either online or in person. When attendees are present, ask them all to take action at the same time and confirm when they have done it. People are more likely to take action and subscribe, rate and review when they are amongst others doing the same.

Create a *WhatsApp* support group -

WhatsApp allows you to bring together up to 256 people in a single group. Messages are sent to each phone at the same time so you know that each person has received the request to take action. Bring the group together a few days before your podcast goes live and ask that they check in with the group when they have taken action.

Create a new *Facebook* group -

use your launch as an opportunity to build an online community. This will be useful for developing conversations with your listeners and gaining useful feedback for your show.

Run competitions –

offer prizes connected to the theme of your show. If you can reward everyone who supports you with a free gift and a special prize for someone who goes the extra mile, you'll achieve more success. There are services to help you compile the contest results such as *Glean.io*. Trainings on the best ways to do this are inside *The Podcast Membership*.

During my launch week I did countless live videos across all of my social media channels and created numerous *audiograms* for each episode in one-minute snippets. Audiograms are videos with a still image (usually your show's artwork) overlaid with the waveform of the audio, moving across the screen as the audio snippet plays, designed as teaser trailers for your full episode. My preferred company for creating these is *Headliner*. They've just partnered with *Libsyn* so if you create an account you can create the audiograms directly from *Libsyn*.

You can't post too often about your podcast launch and I would recommend using a social media scheduler in the run up to the launch day to avoid having to create every post from scratch once your show goes live. Try *Buffer* or *Hootsuite* to schedule posts to *Twitter*, your *Facebook* page, your *Facebook* profile and *Instagram* all at the same time.

During the week of my successful launch I spent a lot of time creating private conversations in *Messenger* and *WhatsApp*, then tracking the show as it climbed the charts. I sent out three emails as part of the launch - the day before I anticipated it would happen, preparing people to look out and support me; when it first went live; in the early evening the same day. I sent another email the following day thanking people for taking action and sharing the results it had achieved, as well as my hopes that it would go higher, and a further request to take action to subscribe, rate, review and download.

Tracking your chart positions

To monitor how your show is doing visit the *iTunes* categories you entered your show into. With sufficient downloads, ratings and reviews to trigger the system your show may appear in the *New Shows* section. This is not standard, however, and you will have done well to get to this point. Within 48 hours of launching your show it should appear within *Chartable.com*, an excellent site for monitoring how your show is doing across the world. If your show has entered any charts, in any category, in any country, you'll be able to view the progress from there. This can be powerful to share on social media. Once your show has reached the pinnacle of becoming a #1 show, it is ALWAYS a #1 show.

Within a day or so from launch you'll see how

many downloads have been listed by *Libsyn* in the dashboard, with further advanced stats if you pay for a premium account. *Apple Podcasts* and *Spotify* are developing the degree of information available on downloads and subscribers so check the stats in each of those accounts, too.

Launching a podcast and seeing your show rise through the charts is exhilarating. It won't happen without implementing everything in this book – along with hard work, diligent research and a commitment to promoting your podcast. If you'd like further support, templates, worksheets and detailed video trainings on launching, growing and monetizing your show, together with resources on being a valued podcast guest and securing podcast bookings, head over to *www.ThePodcastMembership.com*.

Make sure you let me know about your launch and tag me into your social media when your show goes live. I'll be sure to head over and leave you a review.

Finally, I hope that this book has empowered you to start and launch your podcast. Executed with the right know-how it can be a powerful mechanism to get your message out into the world. Knowing that even one life has been altered by hearing your content is rewarding. People can't be touched and transformed if they can't hear you. Be seen, be heard and be remembered. Position yourself strongly in this fast-growing, influential platform and reach the people who need you. To connect with other podcasters and to promote your show, join my free *Facebook* group *The Podcast Community* *www.facebook.com/groups/ThePodcastCommunity*.

Get the planning right and you will create a solid foundation from which to grow, expand and monetize your podcast, fuelling your business with exactly the kind of clients you want to work with. Don't create any old podcast. Launch a podcast with impact.

Podcast Spotlight

Caroline Strawson, *The Narcissistic Abuse Recovery Podcast*

I wanted to start my podcast to educate, inspire and give hope to victims of the trauma from narcissistic abuse. It's a subject close to my heart.

Since launching my show I've achieved the #1 spot in *iTunes* and invitations to appear on other global summits on this subject. My show has ranked in 26 categories and in over 16 countries globally, alongside celebrities such as Joe Wickes, Ferne Cotton & Jay Shetty.

Anna's support enables me to focus on

what I do best and that's content creation. She took care of all the tech with her podcast production agency which I continue working with. This allowed me to feel confident in launching my podcast knowing I'd got the content and that the right audience was going to see it.

Without Anna's production support I would not have launched my podcast! I just wouldn't have had time.

So far, podcasting has had a big impact on my business. It's increased my reach and audience and I'm getting far more emails and messages. It's increased my positioning within this space.

Have a chat with Anna as she will guide you through everything and give you the confidence to get your podcast out there whilst you focus on your genius zone.

ABOUT THE AUTHOR

Anna Parker-Naples is a #1 bestselling author (*Get Visible: How to Have More Impact, Influence & Income*), multi-award winning entrepreneur, business coach and host of *Entrepreneurs Get Visible* podcast (reaching #1 in the *iTunes* charts, outranking Tony Robbins, Marie Forleo, Amy Porterfield and Gary Vaynerchuk).

She lives in Bedfordshire in the UK with her husband, three children, dog Oscar, the family cat ... and the hamsters.

Anna was told in 2010 that she may never walk again due to a complication in pregnancy. Through *NLP* (Neuro- Linguistic Programming) and mindset work she transformed her physical health, recovered fully and embraced a successful career as a multi-award-winning voice actor. After landing herself on the red carpets in Hollywood whilst being celebrated for her audio work, Anna changed focus and now uses her skills and experience to help other purpose-driven entrepreneurs and creatives to step up and become the go-to expert in their field. She has been featured in numerous mainstream media and speaks internationally on audio and the power of podcasting to increase online and industry visibility.

She is CEO of *The Podcast Membership* & her own podcast production agency, and mentors other high-level entrepreneurs in her mastermind programmes.

'Anything's possible when you get visible'

Find out more about Anna

Website: www.annaparkernaples.com
www.ThePodcastMembership.com
Facebook Group:
www.facebook.com/group/ThePodcastCommunity
Resources & Free Downloads
Launch Your Podcast Checklist:
www.annaparkernaples.co.uk/podcastchecklist
10 Steps to Start Your Podcast Guide
www.annaparkernaples.co.uk/10-steps-to-start-your-podcast-2/

facebook.com/AnnaParkerNaplesCoach
twitter.com/annaparkernaple
instagram.com/annaparkernaples
linkedin.com/in/annaparkernaples

Printed in Great Britain
by Amazon